Stories
from the Magic Canoe
of Wa'xaid

Stories from the
MAGIC CANOE
of Wa'xaid

Cecil Paul, as told to Briony Penn

RMB

Originally published in 2019 by RMB | Rocky Mountain Books Ltd.
Copyright © 2020 by Cecil Paul (Wa'xaid) and Briony Penn
Preface copyright © 2020 by Roy Henry Vickers
Foreword copyright © 2020 by Louisa Smith
First Softcover Edition

For information on purchasing bulk quantities of this book, or to obtain media excerpts or invite the author to speak at an event, please visit rmbooks.com and select the "Contact" tab.

RMB | Rocky Mountain Books Ltd.
rmbooks.com
@rmbooks
facebook.com/rmbooks

Cataloguing data available from Library and Archives Canada
ISBN 9781771603379 (softcover)
ISBN 9781771602952 (hardcover)
ISBN 9781771602969 (electronic)

Original cover art by Roy Henry Vickers

Printed and bound in Canada by Friesens

We would like to also take this opportunity to acknowledge the traditional territories upon which we live and work. In Calgary, Alberta, we acknowledge the Niitsitapi (Blackfoot) and the people of the Treaty 7 region in Southern Alberta, which includes the Siksika, the Piikuni, the Kainai, the Tsuut'ina and the Stoney Nakoda First Nations, including Chiniki, Bearpaw, and Wesley First Nations. The City of Calgary is also home to Métis Nation of Alberta, Region III. In Victoria, British Columbia, we acknowledge the traditional territories of the Lkwungen (Esquimalt, and Songhees), Malahat, Pacheedaht, Scia'new, T'Sou-ke and WSÁNEĆ (Pauquachin, Tsartlip, Tsawout, Tseycum) peoples.

We acknowledge the financial support of the Government of Canada through the Canada Book Fund and the Canada Council for the Arts, and of the province of British Columbia through the British Columbia Arts Council and the Book Publishing Tax Credit.

Contents

Adventure Canada trip, Kitlope, June 5, 1993. Left to right:
Ken Hall, James Robertson, Cecil Paul, Roy Henry Vickers.
ANDY MACKINNON

Preface

ROY HENRY VICKERS

Many years ago, I was honoured to travel with Cecil to Kitlope Lake. It was there I heard him tell me the story of T'ismista, the stone hunter. Cecil spoke of stories as a warm wind blowing.

The Magic Canoe brings peace to one's soul. It is a warm wind moving our hearts. Wa'xaid takes us on a journey that regenerates and empowers us. T'ismista, the stone hunter, looks down on the Magic Canoe and reminds us to listen to storytellers like Cecil Paul.

The white down floating in the air is from the Peace Dancer, the Hilikala, who dances the dance of peace spreading eagle down in the big house. The Magic Canoe has Cecil's crest, Killer Whale, at the helm, and Eagle, Raven and Wolf paddling.

I created the original canoe design back in the 1980s, and it was originally titled *Supernatural Visitors*. It seems like this creation was always for my friend Cecil Paul.

This is a story for the family of man; we are all in the canoe together and our stories need to be shared with each other.

November 2018

Foreword

LOUISA SMITH

Nos'ta – I'm listening

Cecil Paul Sr. is not only my beloved big brother who stepped into our late father's shoes at a very young age, but he is also a friend, a huge support, and most of all he is my spiritual guide. He has inspired me, and many others, in his recovery from that age-old, baffling malady, alcoholism. "No other kind of bankruptcy is like this one." He has brushed himself off from this illness and has regained his inborn humbleness in two folds, by reclaiming his spiritual teachings through storytelling and reconnecting to his spiritual being, a birthright. His invisible umbilical cord is firmly attached to Mother Earth.

Storytelling is a way of life for our family. It is a means of teaching through entertainment, education and cultural preservation, as well as instilling moral values. *Nuusa1* ("storytelling") and *nos'ta* ("I'm listening, I hear you") go hand-in-hand during all forms of narratives. If we forget to say "*Nos'ta,*" the storyteller simply stops the story until the next evening, which instills in the listener the necessity of listening attentively to hear the intent/moral of the story. *Nuyem* ("is just the way it is," "it is the law").

More than once I was distracted, and our grandmother, the storyteller, simply stopped in midsentence. She didn't scold me, but my older siblings reinforced my need to listen-up in order to hear the full story. The voiced Ah-ha moment was an indicator that the listener now had the moral of the story imprinted in his or her mind. All other listeners were now inspired to have their Ah-ha moments, and the attention was heightened as a result.

The meaning within the stories is not always explicit, and the listeners are expected to make their own meaning of the stories. Stories function as a tool to pass on knowledge, promote self-awareness, correct inappropriate behaviours or thinking, and promote cooperation. Traditional principles are practised as a way of life.

Cecil, as a storyteller, was in awe when he was invited to California, where he was awarded an Environment Achievement Award and was asked to speak among all the learned scholars, environmentalists, lawyers, teachers and so on. After listening to Cecil speak on the interconnectedness of all living things on Mother Earth, the audience was left in awe of the depth of spiritual knowledge Cecil portrayed in his speech. A similar experience happened when Cecil was invited to the Indigenous House of Learning in Winnipeg to speak to upcoming environmental students. Again, he was among learned scholars who all spoke on the same topic. The students were asked to give a grade to each of the presenters, and to Cecil's surprise, he got the highest grades, mostly As. It was difficult for Cecil to fathom this experience. He was mystified.

Cecil's Magic Canoe was a vision that came to him while contemplating how to save our ancestors' sacred land of

Kitlope Lake from being logged. He saw many hands reaching down from the sky to his outstretched hands while sitting in a canoe on the lake. Sure enough, many hands, people's hands came aboard his canoe to paddle in the same direction to save the Kitlope: loggers, environmentalists, the premier of BC, government officials, the Steelhead Society and many more all came aboard!

The canoe is magic and can hold anyone who wants to come on board. Cecil's open invitation to Kitlope Lake is, "You are welcome to experience the beauty and the sacredness of my beloved land. All I ask is that you leave it intact, as you found it."

Introduction

Lä göläs' – Put your canoe ashore and rest

The Place of My Birth:
"They call it the Kitlope"

My name is Wa'xaid, given to me by my people. *Wa* is "the river"; *Xaid* is "good" – good river.[1] Sometimes the river is not good. I am a Xenaksiala; I am from the Killer Whale Clan. I would like to walk with you in Xenaksiala lands.[2] Where I will take you is the place of my birth. They call it the Kitlope.[3] It is called Xesdu'wäxʷ (Huschduwaschdu) for the "blue, milky, glacial water." Our destination is what I would like to talk about, and a boat – I call it my Magic Canoe. It is a magical canoe because there is room for everyone who wants to come into it to paddle together. The currents against it are very strong, but I believe we can reach that destination, and this is the reason for our survival.

When you leave Kitamaat, this is Haisla Land,[4] you go out to – they call it – Gardner Canal.[5] You go into Gardner, and Crab River is where our boundary line was before the amalgamation of the Xenaksiala and the Haisla.[6] Haisla and Xenaksiala share the same language, with a few word differences. Our language is close to the language family of River's Inlet.[7] You can get the Haisla history from Gordon Robinson.[8]

When I bring the boat into Xenaksiala land, the tide will bring us through. There is a story for that. From Crab River we enter the Kitlope Valley. The Kitlope has many, many rooms, many doors – there is a lot of history going up to Kitlope Lake. Kitlope Lake, if we manage to journey that far, it is what I call the cathedral – a spiritual place.[9] It is quiet. I think if you experience something when we get there, our people say that you will not leave that place unchanged. You cannot leave the way that you went in. Something touches you. Something grabs within you that you never identified as yours, but something in there reveals a little of who we are.

When we get to the Kitlope, I am going to ask you to wash your eyes. Our story says that though you may have 20/20

"It was a magical canoe because there was room for everyone who wanted to come into it to paddle together." Haisla youth in canoe, 2004.
SAM BEEBE, ECOTRUST

Waterfalls, Gardner Canal, May 2015.
GREG SHEA, MAPLE LEAF ADVENTURES

vision or glasses that improve your vision, we are still blind to lots of things. We are blind to Mother Earth. When you bathe your eyes in the artery of Mother Earth that is so pure, it will improve your vision to see things. I will also ask you to wash your ears, so you could hear what goes on around you. So, I could hear you talk. I could hear the wind, and you can hear the birds and animals. If you have the patience to listen, to hear the songs of the birds early in the morning, all these things will be open to you.

We are so busy, we don't have the time for all these beautiful things. If you have the willingness and courage to do that, you will see little things that you have never seen before. You will take a better look at your children, your grandchildren, your best friend. You'll say, "Oh, I never saw that before." To get that vision back – and when you get that back – you will be more kind to whoever comes in your path on this journey. There are many legends that we talk about to our children, and above all, the people around the universe that came with their love and compassion to save something that is known around the world – the largest unlogged temperate rainforest in the world.[10]

Cecil Paul, 2017.
CALLUM GUNN

So Many Arrows Came our Way

1792–1941

I bring my children and grandchildren to the Kitlope every year, starting when I was well.[11] I try to teach them where I was born and teach them about the beauty of the place. Much of what I say was taught to me by my grandmother, my grandfather and my uncles. My late grandmother, Annie Paul, was the leader of our people.[12] She was the matriarch of our family. We were dying off so fast due to foreign diseases that when industry came in there was only a few of us left.[13]

Granny was the first to speak in the negotiation with the chief and council of the Haisla [Kitamaat Band] to amalgamate with the Kitlope Band. The Kitamaat Band welcomed us for amalgamation on March 10, 1948.[14] Amalgamation took place four years before Alcan moved into Kemano territory.[15] We tried to protect our homeland the best way we know how. My people have done it for 10,000 years. With the power of our Creator, we can guard it and keep it the way it is today.

On amalgamation, there was only a few Xenaksiala left. It was Granny who feared that we'd lose everything. The amalgamation was done by the Indian agent. He was stationed in Bella Coola. The document states: "This was a proposal that had been under discussion for considerable time. The only opposition was from the Chief of the Kitlope who did not want to relinquish his somewhat imaginary authority."[16] How do you trust this Indian agent who wrote that? For him to say the "somewhat imaginary authority" was wrong. The chief of the Kitlope had the authority to serve not himself but the people. The opposite of the Canadian government's way of thinking.

My brother, Joe, is on the amalgamation document. He signed it the day we amalgamated – 1948. Gerald, Bruce and I were born a few years too late. It was my friend Charlie Shaw that got the papers from the archives.[17] When I got really sick, I burned a lot of papers, and I had those papers on the census and amalgamation in my hand, and something tells me, *Hang on to this one.* I hang on without knowing and waiting. I had it in my hand, and I thought I wasn't going to make the year. Maybe I was waiting for you.

The story of why we amalgamated is told in the census papers,[18] where the government said: "How many Indians left in the 'concentrations camps' at Kitlope?" How many? 30 people. What year? 1934. Kitlope Reserve. In the column "Under 7 years," it says "Male: 2." One is me; the other is my brother. When I sat down and first saw that document, my wife came down and she sees tears in my eyes. "*Doo'tii ƚl'sin'la.* Tell me what those tears are for?"

In our verbal history, according to my little[19] granny and all the chiefs, each one of them said: "We numbered over 700." I heard some stories. When I close my eyes, I go back to the teaching of my three Elders. I asked them: "*G'in c'äquëlas?* How many of us Xenaksiala?" And they all came out to – not the same number – but close, eh. "*G'in c'äquëlas?* How many?"

When you begin to hear this story…the three of them told me, "*Lä'k'äi.* It's past…seven."

"Oh, seven hundred?" I say.

"*K'ew x^wenox^w gai'pen'xiidii kä.* No, my child, it is more than

20

that." They mentioned all their villages.[20] They didn't live in one village like today – a reserve here and there.

"In those days," my uncle told me, "just around Kitlope Lake alone there's four villages, five clans: the Raven, Killer Whale, Eagle, and the Beaver." Used to be Salmon and Wolf too. Look at what they are telling me: "*Aqua'ain goam sü wiixäi.* White man has come."

I believe it was the Indian agent who came and distributed blankets to the chiefs and people, and they were contaminated. Our stories said that they gave away infected blankets. They called them "ugly" blankets: *Ya'yak'sta.* At that time the government had a chemical warfare to get rid of the Indians. When I found that out years later in Bella Bella, I went to Winnipeg; I asked the chiefs. What happened? In Queen Charlottes, that chief – who was in Alberni too and a really good friend of mine – he brought me to Skedans. That whole village was wiped out. Not one person left. But when he brought me there, there was a lot of totem poles. Some standing, lots on the ground. All die of this disease. So, it went right across Canada, this chemical warfare on how to kill an Indian.[21]

When they were mapping out the reservations, the government sent a guy out to tell the Haisla what their reservation is going to be.[22] Our big chief told him, "*Wa'wais*" – the mountaintops where the first little stream starts from the mountain and comes down to our valley, to the hot spring. All the way down the channel as far as Butedale and all the way up to the headwaters of the Kitimat. As big chief, he knew all the boundary lands of different *wa'wais*, down the coast and further back. "That's home. That's all our place."[23]

And the chiefs try to tell this guy [the surveyor], they ask: "Who was speaking for the Haisla?"

And that guy didn't listen. He wrote to the Indian agent: "The Haisla had 35 acres," and he described this village. "This place here, you can't cultivate it. Couldn't plant nothing, it's all rocks. There's a little stream coming down, that's the one you cross and either side of the river is rows of wild crab apples, *which the Indians like*. Your obedient servant."

That whole valley of people, the Haisla people with the oolichan fishing,[24] only got a small little portion of Haisla land where they grew up, but that whole valley was Haisla. The chief asked: "What is this 35 acres of rocky soil? Concentration camp for Haisla people?" This was just a summer camp; they didn't understand that. Kitlope was no different. That was when you start to mistrust. I've often wondered what would have happened if some guy had written back: "Nobody's going to educate the Indian. We got a few crab apples. Your obedient servant."

There was a bad friction between the Indian agent and the chiefs. They told him, "You can't have that, that's our home. Why are they putting this reservation there?" But our people didn't know what was happening. They had a sense that these people were bad. There was an argument. And from Victoria, they had a war ship called *Clio*, which came and anchored there. Now it is Clio Bay. Was it to quiet the Natives down? I don't really know.[25]

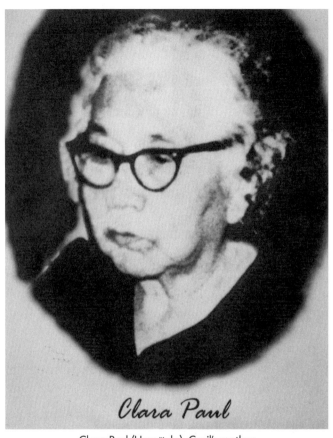

Clara Paul (Hayxʷaks), Cecil's mother.
CECIL PAUL FAMILY

Thomas (Tom) Paul,
Cecil's father c. 1936.
CECIL PAUL FAMILY

Annie Paul, Wiïdealh,
Wa'xaid's 'little Granny.'
No date.
CECIL PAUL FAMILY.

Annie Paul, the queen of my family, 96 years old when she died. Her husband is Chief Johnny Paul, Chief Humzeed. My mother Clara, who holds the title of the great chief lady, which my brother Dan held, Chief G'psgolox.[26] And that is her husband who is the Killer Whale Clan chief, Thomas Paul, my father. He was only 42 years old when he died of tuberculosis. Very young. My auntie, his sister, died too, only 40. My brother, Leonard – they talk about the Miller Bay Hospital – that is where my brother died in the TB hospital in Prince Rupert, only 20 years old.

A year and a half later, after Leonard passed away, the miracle drug they called streptomycin came in. All the hospitals were filled with my people – Miller Bay, Coqualeetza, Nanaimo – all army and air force hospitals, were filled with Indian people with tuberculosis. Inside one year when streptomycin came in to hospitals, a miracle happened. Wish my brother had lived long enough to see the miracle happen. I praise society for coming up with something to penetrate that thing that tuberculosis has – the germ. No other drug would penetrate that to arrest what took my people.[27]

Now only four of us left – four full-blooded Xenaksiala people. Three ladies: my little sisters Louisa[28] and Vietta, and Lillian Henry, my cousin. Now, out of 700 or more, you're sitting across from the only male left from Kitlope. Kemano cemetery is where I am going to be when I go to sleep. So many arrows came our way.[29]

Journey in the Magic Canoe

1990–1994

Survey Markers:
These Ribbons Are Sharper than Arrows

I will start my story during my healing journey. I took my sister Louisa, my little sister Vietta, their children and three or four of mine to the Kitlope. That's when I repeat my story to them of where I was born, what I'd done, the joy, and where to go and play. When we landed there this time, there was survey markers.[30] Something I'd never seen there. I went to go take a look. I walked the length of our little homestead, and there was a cedar tree standing there. I saw this tree where my granny would take a little bit of the bark in May and April, when the sap is running. She made this box from the cedar bark, enough to hold 24 fish; that's how she counted the fish in the box to put away. That's what she got from that tree, and she don't touch that tree no more. She only take that much, and the tree is alive. When I got there, the tree had survey markers with black numbers. "Oh, this is bad." I went back to Kitamaat. Instead of spending five days that I promised the children, I come back here to Kitamaat on the second day. I said: "These survey markers are what I dread. These ribbons are sharper than arrows. They will cut deeper than knives." I knew logging was coming, but not this soon. They were survey markers to put a road into where? It was going to go through where I was born.

For a moment, I was hesitant, you know. I was concerned about my family. I worked for the company [Eurocan / West Fraser] in Kitimat,[31] before they applied for a tree-farm licence for the Kitlope. I want you to know I am not against all industry. It is how they take the resources out of our sacred land that

Cecil Paul's cabin site on the Kitlope River,
and redcedars to which survey markers were tied.
BRIONY PENN

is Wa'xaid's concern. I saw what happened with West Fraser, the destruction around all the clear-cut logging, and now they got approval from the government for their tree-farm licence to log in Kitlope. I told my wife, "I am going to fight for this place. We might lose our house. Our kids are going to high school and need all them things for school. The company that has the tree-farm licence, I am working for."

My wife Mae said, "No, you go ahead. I'll walk with you." And that is all I wanted to hear: "I'll walk with you." And that was the beginning.

Launch a Supernatural Canoe

I told Gerald Amos,[32] an elected chief who had become more of a son to me – a brother – and our hereditary chief, Simon Hall,[33] that, "I'm going to put my life on the line for this. I'm going to go fast for four days. After six to eight days, come looking for me, in case I have a [motor] breakdown."

I went up on the riverbank by the tree of my little granny. I hear my granny's spirit: "*Masi sax qasüüs?* What are you here for?"

I tell her, "Because they are going to destroy, they are going to kill the Kitlope, our valley."

"In my dream, there will be a lot of people coming to help," she says. "You launch a supernatural canoe and no matter who comes aboard to help us save the Kitlope, *gän'im łlaka'tlee* – there will be lots of paddlers – that canoe would never be filled. Take a person that will guide you through uncharted waters to save the Kitlope."

I stayed another two days, and I had my answer from the tree. Gerald, sister Louisa and I in the canoe, because Louisa was there when I picked up the survey marker. She was there from day one.

In my dream, my little granny asks me, "*Un'gwai dlä lä xl ɬli?* Who is going to be chief at the front of the canoe?" She didn't give me an answer, but I thought about it and put it on the table.

"I would like to nominate Gerald Amos to be our leader and spokesman. He understands more about the adopted language than any of us put together. He will speak for us." Went around the table, everyone nodded their head. I said, "*Nooxʷ dla lä xiila.* I'll steer the boat and be in the stern to see where we are going." We were in uncharted waters and each time I always had Gerald in the front of the canoe. When you're on the river, he's the one in the front that looks after everybody's safety. Gerald was our spokesman. My sister is in the middle. Sometimes the river is so wide, and she'd instruct. We all agreed.

I went back to my hereditary chief. Our hereditary chief says, "Go on that journey, but ask the other chiefs."

I asked every one of them, "Will you walk with Wa'xaid in my journey, in the Kitlope?" I said to my sister Louisa, "*Ai'go 'la 'gliss ka'tla.* We've got to walk softly. We've been hurt and damaged so many times." I thought about my brothers in the union:[34] What are they going to do? Am I taking their bread and butter for fighting for what I believe in? Fighting for the Kitlope? For my people?

I have three paddlers now, four with the hereditary chief. Four clans said that they were in, and the canoe was filling up. The hereditary chief asked Gerald, "Do we have any funding in the kitty to get our people together?"

Gerald said, "Yes. Pick the day inside one week from today." Gerald called all the people together. I told my grandchildren to get a few of the survey markers and then stay four or five days in Kitimat. The beginning of the battle started there.

Referendum: 98 per cent Said They Would Walk with Me

We had a feast; a bunch of people were there. I had one of my grandchildren bring the story of the survey markers up in front of the people. The hereditary chief told the people what these survey markers are, and I told them where they had come from. I told them, "I consider it not only my home, but it's a bank for us. It's a bank for our people. From logging this valley, they're going to destroy all the species of the Pacific salmon that come here. We are going to have nothing to eat if we let this happen. What's going to happen to the deer and the moose, the bear, the oolichan, the things we harvest from this bank? This bank is threatened. What are we going to do?" We had a little referendum in the village here: 98 per cent said they would walk with me. I don't know who the 2 per cent were. Best for me not to know.

The Boston Men

Then I got a call from Gerald. He asked, "Are you well to travel?" At that time, I had had a massive heart attack. He said, "Some environmentalists wanted to meet with us in Vancouver."

I said, "Let's go to Vancouver."

We met two young men of Ecotrust America.[35] These environmentalists had an office in Portland. And we met these two and a beautiful friendship developed. We called them Boston Men. Didn't know who they were, and they asked if they could be of help. "Can your canoe get a little bigger Cecil/ Wa'xaid? Can you bring more people?"

I said, "Yeah, that thing will hold anybody that wants to come aboard."

One of the things that was asked: "Do we trust these Americans?"

"Kitlope crew," c. 1993. Left to right: Spencer Beebe,
Cecil Paul, Gerald Amos, Bruce Hill, Yvon Chouinard.
SAM BEEBE, ECOTRUST

I said, "This canoe, Gerald, we're going to teach them to paddle in rhythm. Let's not fight one another."

I got to Vancouver late that night, and we were supposed to meet with them, 8:30 in the morning. I went to sleep, and I dreamt of a cloud and there was hands coming down and the hands were almost touching but there was no connection. And there was a bang, and Gerald woke and said, "Come on partner, it's time to go. We're going to be late for these guys."

I said, "Gerald, come here. You just spoiled a beautiful dream. It should have never ended."

Gerald said, "Come on, hurry up, let's go."

That's the first time I met Spencer Beebe. I take a look at this guy and he looked at his partner [Ken Margolis] and they introduced themselves and sat down. He said, "We're on a journey to find out what's left of the rainforests in the world."

"Our satellite," they said, "stops in the Kitlope, and scientists, who take these images, have communicated that if no logging has started, we'll be the second largest rainforest watershed in the world that has never been logged."

Gerald called a little later. "How are you feeling, Brother? These Americans are coming. They are going to fly into the Kitlope. They gave me the date. Who should I call to come along?"

I said, "Our new member, Charlie Shaw. He's a good person when the journey is rough. When you've been standing too long without taking a step to get out of this mess we are in, he will crack a joke. He'll make us laugh a while and come back to our business." That is why Charlie was with us all through the journey.

Charlie Shaw. He married a full-blooded Kitlope girl. I told Charlie a little bit. I talk about this American we're going to meet. "I don't know them," I said, "but it's a journey to save the Kitlope."

Charlie said, "What time do we go?" That's the fifth one in the canoe from this village, and we went there to see the Americans and some funny things happened.

Charlie Shaw, Gerald Amos, Cecil Paul, c. 1993.
SPENCER B. BEEBE, ECOTRUST

The day we got to where we were supposed to rendezvous in the Kitlope, I see somebody waving on the beach. Charlie told the captain, "Pretend not to see them." We drove by in the boat where these guys were, and they turned around to watch us. None of them had dry clothes. We went on and had a big fire at the place where I was born.

Spencer looked at Gerald and me and said, "I'd like to make an apology to you. Remember I told you in Vancouver it was the second-largest untouched temperate rainforest? It's been confirmed. The scientists say it's the largest."

We were in the canoe that we were going to paddle. I told Spencer, "Your education, your science is far beyond what little I have or Gerald. If we're going to work together, I don't want nothing said to the media without our consent. We have to see what you – with your mind – think Kitlope should do to stop the logging, and we will honour you if you do the same. If we're going to be partners in this canoe, we'll have to work together. We've got to be in harmony and paddle together." There was a handshake, and that was good.

What we were fighting was big industries that have lawyers and all that. I don't understand their language very well, so we were up against something so BIG. Then the guys brought in the scientists; bird scientists, river scientists, all kinds of scientists, come help us save the Kitlope. I had a wounded spirit and sometimes I said, "I want to give up." But a little child would come to me and say, "Don't stop now. Maybe there will be a door that opens."

Dr. John: Right from the Heart

By this time of the journey, I was ill. My heart was not good then, and I'm not allowed to travel with them to meet the company that is logging. I told the both of them: "Gerald, bring your regalia along." I says, "I don't know who you are going to meet, but something tells me you'll need it." I said, "Get one for Dr. [John] Pritchard;[36] tell my daughter to give him mine. We'll adopt him in our clan." Before that, he was the first non-Native that was adopted in Haisla land, and he was adopted into the Eagle Clan. You cannot be accepted by the Great Spirit if your own clan doesn't [accept you], but the two hereditary chiefs agreed. That was awesome. To baptize a white person that I mistrusted with that seed of hatred? I'm healing, you know. I remember in that big hall, when I gave him his name. I told him, "They will drum, and I'll knock my hand, and you'll go and dance. Dance around the place. Go to the hereditary chief – you stop and you bow to him. Don't move for a few seconds. If he gets up and they come and pat you on the shoulder you are accepted in Haisla." He bowed his head to the chief, and John got up, big smile on his face. John flew around, never danced before in his life. But he almost took off in the air. It came to him, right from the heart.

Bruce Hill: He Put His Power Saw Away

There is a little river in the Kitlope valley called Wow'kst where only two kinds of salmon go: the steelhead in April, and September the coho. I followed the survey markers; it went right across the spawning beds for the steelhead, and I told

Gerald, "You got to tell people: don't touch anywhere near the survey markers. Whoever is going to come volunteer from the Steelhead Society or sportsmen, we got to show them that this spawning bed would be no more if they log." That is why I said, "We got to invite them – they could be our greatest allies. Get them inside this Magic Canoe, Gerald. They are going to help us paddle."

And then we brought up the vice-president of the Steelhead Society, Bruce Hill.[37] He was a logger, this guy – very sarcastic guy. We went up there to that little creek. Up there we began to talk sensibly. I said, "If you allow that logging, it is going to destroy the fish. Only two species come up this way: coho and steelhead." I brought him right up to the big hole by the water-fall. The fish don't go any further. It is the end of their journey. On the right-hand side is a big, deep hole. My Elders, years ago, had a long pole of cedar, very light, and they tied the end of the net over it and speared the fish inside the deep pool.

I try to trace back to that time when I was able to talk to Bruce as a friend without anger. He would say, "Get that damn net out of the water," and that kind of language. Now we could talk with no anger in the voice. I tell him, "We are in uncharted waters, your life and mine." I try to reach inside, that's the only way I know how. "Understand what that little creek is going to do, an artery of Mother Earth. How are we going to protect it together? It isn't just steelhead. I'm trying to give you an idea, a vision of how Wa'xaid done it."

How do I reach out and tell him that I am fighting all these years? How do I reach into Bruce's spirit and make him understand? Damaging a valley through clear-cut logging. He was a faller, vice-president of Steelhead. You got to talk softly. Talk softly with them. Let them come here and see what the valley means. Bruce put his power saw away and he came aboard the canoe, and then for a while he helped with Rediscovery Camps[38] and got the Nanakila Institute started with Spencer. They both were white men. I hear this beautiful laughter of my friend, Bruce Hill. You can pick up his laughter from far away; it sounds good. I don't know where he is, but I recognize that laugh. I heard it in the Kitlope. I'll always remember this gentleman. Good journey.

Haisla kids from Rediscovery Camp,
Nanakila Institute, Kitlope Lake, c. 1993.
BRIAN FALCONER

Brian Falconer: Big White Magic Canoe

The people that came aboard this canoe were something beautiful because of the love of the environment. One of them was a captain of the sailboat vessel *Maple Leaf*[39] who was in the fight with us for years. The captain said, "I love the environment. I take people out to BC, and they are all environmentalists." He said, "Maybe we could be of help?" That was music to my ears. The offer gave me the energy to take another step. I met the captain of this boat, and his name was Brian Falconer. A journey with this man was something awesome and beautiful. My brother said he wanted to show me something – he wants to show me what the Creator wants me to enjoy. He was the first one in a big boat that brought people up to my place of birth. He told his crew, "You are going to the largest untouched rainforest in the universe." It is the first sailboat to come and help us try and save the Kitlope. The amazing part of it is, when I tell my story to the children, I am touched at how many of them were interested.

Discovery

One day Brian Falconer says, "Cecil, I have a special guest out on the boat who I'd like you to meet."

And I say, "Yes." His special guest is an elderly man from Victoria, Dick Wells,[40] and he is going to have Brian follow the route of Captain Vancouver surveying the ocean. I heard the story of Vancouver many times. Johnny Wilson and I, we used to go and try to learn our culture, our history. And we would go to the old lady, Louise Barbettis's granny,[41] and she told the

Maple Leaf under ice-capped mountains
in Gardner Canal, May 2015.

GREG SHEA   MAPLE LEAF ADVENTURES

story three times to Johnny and I. We listened. We didn't tell her we'd heard it before – the story when we first encountered Europeans. That's what really got me. I close my eyes and I see this storyteller and her granny telling her. How many centuries ago? And then the guy, Dick Wells, who wrote the book on Captain Vancouver, brings that story. I said, "Read it to me, Brian. Read it slow." Every word in the written form was the same as the verbal history of the Haisla.[42] Every word. Verbal culture … every word. I went to take the book to that old lady and told her granddaughter to read. "Read it really slow," I said. "*Sii lü ka'ppa?*" she asked. "Is it right?"

It is amazing. It is exactly how the white man wrote it, that the Indians traded two 80-pound fish.[43] The Indians were sitting there, and one told his chief, "There's a bunch of ants running around." It was their hats. They had railings like Brian's sailboat and just their heads were seen from the canoe way down in the harbour. It was a bunch of ants in this new island. But it was a sailboat named *Discovery*, and that is our history – what they see.

Each chief had a lieutenant. There was this one guy called Thloxw. Not afraid of anything, he never leaves the side of his hereditary chief. He put his life in battle. And the chief told him, "See what those children are worried about." Thloxw goes to investigate what the children saw and comes back again and told the chief what he saw. "Did you go close?" he asked.

"*K'ew,*" Thloxw says. "No." He wasn't afraid. He was groomed to be fearless and he noticed that the ants – what the people called them – were human beings. Their heads were black.

They met at the first island after leaving Kitamaat (going out on the left-hand side), Kildala.[44] We know exactly where that is. Must have happened in springtime? Maybe in May? They brought spring salmon, so it had to be in the springtime.

Rediscovery

The world came – all these people coming to experience the uncharted waters of Kitlope. To leave their loved ones at home, to come and help us to push our cause, leaves me in awe. Without the help of these people across the border, we would be still fighting today. They all became good friends of Kitlope.[45] My new friends said, "I will walk with you."

I replied, "You will not leave Kitlope unchanged."

There were three young ladies with two young men, and they were students from University of Toronto, and they journeyed across here when they heard about the fight. Made their own way. It was a beautiful day and the mountains were clear and they gave me coffee, and I said, "Let's go down to my land." Who are these kids who come all the way across this beautiful country to save this place?

There was the scientist, Randy Stoltmann,[46] who fell off the rock and he never lived. When the government asked me to go identify the remains for the family, I go to where he fall off, and I sat there for a while. I heard from another book that there is no greater love of man than one who laid his life down for the land. And that was what Randy was. He was a friend of the environment, a friend of the Haisla people, and my brother laid down his life for me. Lot of phone calls. Who are these kids to be swept to Haisla land? Love. It was a heavy price paid for this valley.

I had another environmental sister, Glenn Fuller.[47] She was the Coca Cola heiress, Sweetgrass Foundation. She bought the motor for the punt. Gerald and I took her up to the Kitlope for a month when she was diagnosed for cancer. She died.

Ric Young,[48] he came up to the Kitlope with Ian Gill, Ecotrust. Ric took the story of the Magic Canoe to a big Indigenous conference in Australia. When Ric was in Australia, he met an African chief, and he liked my story of the Magic Canoe. "My friend," he said. "I'd like you to talk to him [Cecil]." They invited me to go to Africa. I don't know why. The doctor said I couldn't go.

Dave Campeche lived near the big river not far from Seattle, and he came up. He was a cook. Owns sort of a restaurant hotel, or motel, they call it. He came and cooked with Rediscovery one year, and we became really good friends. He asked me to come down to Vancouver. He had three boys; two were in jail. I went to go visit them in jail.

One time, Gerald asks, "You got time to go to Vancouver? Americans want to meet with you."

"Okay," I say. "Let's go." It was fundraising for the Kitlope. He said there is going to be celebrities there. We go to the Vancouver Hotel.

Dr. Pritchard is with me when a guy comes. "I know that guy. He is coming to our table," he says. "Have you ever seen his movie?"

"I don't think so," I says.

"It is Harrison Ford,"[49] he says. "Movie star. Goodness sakes – don't tell him you don't know."

And the next one came. What was his name? I don't know the man, but he is with a lady who is a country western singer. I forgot him, but I remember her; I have seen parts of her body before, like Dolly Parton.

With One of the Rockefeller Brothers
I Go to See the White Bear

Then there was the Rockefeller Foundation – the rich people in the States. With one of the Rockefeller brothers I go to see the White Bear.[50] He called me brother. We went up to Johnny Clifton's country in Bernard Harbour,[51] where we anchored the boat – big sailboat. We went ashore up the creek, and he asked, "How come you don't have a camera?"

Rockefeller says, "I'll get you one."

I says, "Get me the cheapest one. Something you just push." He had one of 'em big expensive things, and that's what I got, from Rockefeller. It is still hanging on my door.

He hasn't called for over a year now, used to call all the time. I can't remember his name. Must be David. You know, for rich people to come, meet the people, eat my food, Kitlope food… he loved the [oolichan] grease. Make toast of it in the morning. He'd have toast maybe three times a day. Sometimes in the campfire, I'd take a potato and I'd put really fine sand on part of it. Oh! Take it out, eat it together with the grease. They gave us over $80,000 to buy gas and grub for our Rediscovery kids' camps. They done it with love.

David Rockefeller Jr. and Cecil Paul, kayaking, Kitlope, c. 1993.
SPENCER B. BEEBE, ECOTRUST

What's Left of the Fresh Water in the Universe?

Gerald phoned one day. "Good morning, brother. How you feel today?"

I says, "Not bad. Just about to go out the door when the phone rang."

"Oh, good," he says. "Could you stay another half hour? Someone's going to call you. I think you might like it. Please have patience, eh."

I wait for 45 minutes. "Let's go," I told my wife. Put my coat on, and both of us are by the door. The phone rang. Henning Hesse[52] was on the phone, a scientist from Germany. I took my coat off. "Okay," I said. "What's on your mind?"

He says, "There's three of us. We're scientists, and the

government appointed us to find out what's left of the fresh water in the universe and we're to choose three countries. We got Europe, South America...and we looked at the internet and we see the largest rainforest in the universe."

The three of us talked: "I wonder what it's like there? I wonder if our government would want to see the fresh water that's never been touched by industry? We need a guide to bring us up."

I was healthy then. I says, "Okay."

When they came, my son Cecil Jr. was working as a watchman for Nanakila in the Kitlope. Boat owners took the scientists up, me up. Explained to them everything. They had a cameraman with them, and I took him down to the river. German filmmaker asks, "What does the river mean to you?" I explained it was the artery of Mother Earth. I sang the song that they sang when we brought Granny home. And when, must be a year gone by, when they tried to invite me to Frankfurt, for the film. *Watery Vision* is the name of the documentary. Henning says, *wasser* in German. W-A-S-S-E-R. My doctor says, "too far," for my heart. And I missed the opening of that film: *What's left of the fresh water in the universe?*

Merve Wilkinson: In the Wilderness He Keeps

I met this wonderful person, Merve Wilkinson,[53] and he came up to Kitlope. He called and asked to come. He has a forest not far from Nanaimo, Wildwood. He teaches about selective logging. He wondered why none of the forestry students of the university go and study in the wilderness he keeps. Then he finds out the owners of MacMillan Bloedel are teachers of the university, and they won't allow the young ladies to go and see Merve and how to select logs.

Brian Falconer and I came to his place, and he welcomed us and we walked to a seedling. Merve says, "Cecil, try pull this one." And I couldn't budge it. We walk a little ways to another seedling, and he says, "Now, try that one," and I pulled it out. He says, "That second one is manmade and that is what the foresters are doing. This first one here is our Creator's, the roots are all spread out and you couldn't pull it out. The manmade is straight down and the roots are not developing right, so when you stop and think about it – between the Creator and the man – how wrong we are."

It was amazing for me to meet a person that is educated and come up to the Kitlope. I walked with him and showed him big trees, and then I go to his place where he is trying to show the forest industry, the loggers, about select logging – no logging road, no nothing. Where I was born there was a Douglas fir still standing on the hill; showed it to Merve and how far the tree grows. It don't grow any other place as far north. It is in the book; some scientist wrote it. It is true that there are no more. For me to cross paths with that man, I am very fortunate. I was not well when he passed away. They tried to call me down to say a few words. Brian and I sat with him for hours in his home, discussing these things.

MERVE WILKINSON IN 1995 AT KITLOPE LAKE

Grizzly Bear: He Holds Up Everything

I brought three scientists up to see what I was shown by my Xenaksiala teachers. Grizzly bear, all kinds of grizzly bears and different colours: orange and yellow. They spot at age. Some of them are pitch black; some of them are light brown with white faces. It is very unusual. My people never touch a grizzly bear. They drilled into us when we were young, that he's our friend in the bush. He is my brother; he is a guardian of the forest. All Xenaksialas hold this. The totem, you study the images of what is put down, and always at the bottom is the grizzly bear. He is strong; he holds up everything. What is on the top? The majority of the poles will have the eagle on top. The vision the eagle has is sharp. He's guiding everything above, and you often see that in the Kitlope.

One day, a grizzly hunter guide comes looking for grizzlies, and I heard him say that he would shoot through the Indian children at the camp to kill a grizzly bear. I say to him, "These are not only Haisla children but children from around the world, and you threaten to shoot through the children?" I talked to him by the little creek, "Say to me please, 'I'm sorry.'"

He said, "Wa'xaid, I'm sorry."

But what is he sorry about? He didn't elaborate on that word. Sorry to shoot through that child? Sorry because I met with him? Maybe because I didn't accept the apology? I never met him again after that.[54] We have a word for a type of grizzly that is angry or a killer; it is called *gil dee spa*.

Many Doors Opened for Wa'xaid

Many doors opened for Wa'xaid. In my journey, I think the beauty of it was – and I tell this to the children, and to Elders – I said, "I trust them, I trust them, and that's where the trust begins. We're going to save the Kitlope with a race I hated and distrusted."

Journey of Hell

1941–1971

Wawa lumgila: There Is No Stopping Death When It Comes to Your Door

In Kemano, when you sit in a point across the bay, there is a mountain – there are no trees growing on it. That mountain our people call Ł'loxʷ (Thok): Strong. In the middle of the highest point is one little tree still standing today, and I was brought up there by my uncle. When the world flood came, that mountain was supernatural, *yüü'xm*. The water didn't cover the whole rock, and that little tree is where our people anchored or tied the rope of their canoe around. The canoe was moving back and forth; that is the way the little tree looked. The boy in the bow of the canoe was so weak from not enough to eat that he missed his fish when he speared it. Then out came the hawk, *'tä'ta'kwa*, took the fish by the neck and put it in the canoe. It was the dogfish. It saved the people. That was the first animal that the Creator has given the Xenaksiala people from the ocean. "*Qʷ'a äits*," my uncle says. "Sit down." When the water went down, they see the treetops of Kemano.

My little granny told us that when there was an earthquake there would be a big wave that would raise the canoes. *Wawa lumgila* – there is no stopping death when it comes to your door.[55]

Elizabeth Long Memorial School: I Felt So Alone

I was six years old when I was at this residential school in Kitamaat Village. Elizabeth Long Memorial School.[56] Elizabeth Long was, I guess, the principal or the preacher – United

Church. Young as I was, they had a little window, and I looked out at the channel. I remember lying down there, looking and hoping my dad will come around the point with his boat and pick me up. I am Xenaksiala, and these boys are Haisla, and we didn't get along too well. I felt so alone. I remember that. Later, when I lived and worked in Butedale, steamboats come in. Before the boats come in they blow the whistle, and when they took me to Alberni, I could hear the train whistles just like the ships coming into Butedale. I remember I had tears of loneliness listening to the train whistles, like the steamboats, coming to take me home. It never happened. Same way here when I was six or seven years old, looking at the point: "Come on, Dad. Come, Dad, I am lonesome for you." Never come. Never came.

We had that little football [soccer] team. I am the only one alive now from that picture. Lawrence King, Percy King and Percy Mack in the picture. I think the teaching I got from all that suffering was, I say to all my grandchildren, my children: "I will never leave you. I'll fight for you if I believe you are right."

Everybody Hid Their Children

I talked about the gift of memory, and I think that's the most wonderful thing in my life. Memory was something to hang on to; that there's a good life on the other side of bad. No one can ever steal that from you at any time. It is yours, to hold the beauty of what happened, and somehow the ugliness of things disappears, but the beauty of it remains with you till the end of the day, end of your life.

Cecil Paul and the soccer team from Elizabeth
Long Memorial Home, Kitamaat Village, c. 1938.
Cecil is third from the left in the back row.

I went to my uncle, James Henry, a canoe builder – learned
visually without going to school and self-taught – and that is
where I was directed to go by my father. My uncle said, "I'll
take him." Same as the young ladies who went to their aunties
to learn how to cut fish and get things from the trees and cedar
and what roots to take to make baskets, that kind of schooling.
That was our system in the Kitlope until my grandfather took
me [from Elizabeth Long], and I never went back and kept
hiding from the missionaries in the Kitlope. It was a truth that
everybody hid their children and didn't know what to expect.

Dr. Peter Kelly came up to Kitlope a whole lot of times before I went to Alberni.[57] I told my little granny: the chief's [Dr. Kelly's] wife is beautiful. He used Chinook language and little granny didn't speak English, and how at ease they were with my grandfather and grandmother, and I remember him. He was well respected.

It was 1937 or 38 because after that we went to Kemano and Kitlope and stayed there. Kitlope is where my grandfather hid me from that residential school. I used to pack his bait to the trapline. I'd make a little fire by the river. "*Kä kwa däs* – Listen," Grandfather says. "The river is singing a song to us." You could hear one river go over a rock like this, and it will make a different sound, smaller one that is bass, alto and soprano. "The river is singing to us, if you stop and listen," he says. I remember hearing that. If it weren't for him, I wouldn't know that the river talks to us, making the different sounds. It has been a long time since I have been out quietly sitting by a river.

The stories I received, at maybe eight and nine, I remember well. At that age, I travelled with my grandfather, looking over his trapline. I saw him at that age bring down a deer with a bow and arrow. In my short life on this earth, I also see footprints in the moon. Humans went far beyond our land, Mother Earth. And it goes too fast for Wa'xaid, this life. What did I do? I did a lot of many things. I was taught how to trap, how to respect the bear and other animals. I was taught that we live together in this wilderness with the animals. Take what we need.

It was at that time when I was first told the importance of water. They told us when we go hunting to bathe in the water, and my grandfather would add devil's club that I would wash myself in.[58] I would smell of the wilderness, and if I didn't bathe I wouldn't have the pleasure of going with them on a hunting trip. When you smell of the devil's club it has an odour that's beautiful. When you walk around the bush you could smell this same odour. If the wind is not in your favour and it blows towards the animal, it will run away if you don't bathe in it.

These little teachings I got from him endured for me in my life. The joy of a sunrise and the sunset. I remember asking my mother about the four seasons: winter, spring, summer, fall – each one of the four seasons is a time to harvest, a time to prepare for the winter months when you can't travel too much. Prepare for the winter. But then with the residential schools, if no leader is prepared to defend the nation, they laid down: "Do whatever you want." That is when the death of the culture could come. We died slowly; we were conquered.

Devil's club, Kitlope, May 2015.
GREG SHEA, MAPLE LEAF ADVENTURES

Alberni: The Journey of Hell Begins

That was a joyous time in my life on the Kitlope; it was beautiful. I never knew when I was nine years old that one day I would lose the teachings of my Elders. At age ten and a half, my friends and I were playing on the hillside, and we went to an opening and looked down on the riverbank, see the boat come in. I heard a new motor coming, stopped on my beach. There was three of them on the boat. I learned years later it was the Indian agent representing Canada. Another one with a uniform was the provincial police. They came to pick me up. Someone told the Indian agent where I was, and they came up and picked me up in the Kitlope. Came right up the Kitlope River. Children at that age are kind of curious. Wondering what happened to my grandfather and grandmother, I went right down to the beach, looked out, and there was some strangers who stayed in the background and watched. He was instructed to remove children and take them to a residential school. My little granny said: "*Waa daa nox^w!* Don't look back, my son. Don't look back." Why did little Granny say, "Don't look back?" I think it was because she was powerless to help. Those words are what was said when people had no choice, if they were captured in warfare. I could hear my mum crying sometimes...lonesome.

It happened to me with a few other children. At the age of ten and a half, I journeyed from the Kitlope, leaving my things, my granny, my mum and grandfather. It was years later I learned where we ended up at. It was a residential school in a place that was Port Alberni, Vancouver Island.[59] The journey of hell begins when I was ten, when they took me away from my family. That was the beginning of hell for a ten-year-old that didn't understand a word of English. I stayed four years in this Port Alberni. I never went home. I had a lot of good friends, especially one, Russell Ross. He's a Haisla and we speak the same language: Xenaksiala and Haisla. My friend just passed away last Christmas. He was 89, four years older than me. There were signs all over – I learned later of the rules – and the one with the most big letters, that YOU ARE NOT TO TALK YOUR MOTHER TONGUE. Russell and I didn't know how to read and were talking in our language.

A big guy came, he had a whistle in his mouth, blowing his whistle. He took me by the collar and my friend, whistling until he got to what they called the playroom. One hundred and seventeen boys. They lined up the boys and circled right around and took me and Russell, took us in the middle of this playroom and asked to remove our trousers. We did. I remember I can still see the weapon they used for me not to talk my mother tongue: a black leather strap. Three feet long maybe, and it was double. One was about an inch, the other was inch and a half. One would hit and the other one would follow. They made an example of us, I learned later. They did the same with each reserve who spoke a different language. We happened to be the ones to be made an example of, my friend and I.

When I knew what was coming I spoke to my friend. I said, "*Kéc'gʷäsa*. Don't cry, brother. Don't cry." We are talking in our language in front of them, my tormentor. I got five more hits.

The third one that hit my rear end, I glanced up at my tormentor and he had a smile, I could still see. And with that smile a seed was planted in my heart. A seed of hatred. A seed of mistrust to my tormentor. My tormentor, I learned later, was run by the United Church of Canada, a white man.[60] They cultivated this hatred so well. Cultivated this mistrust. The hate. What I mean by cultivate is planting hatred in my heart. My friend Russell and I went underground with our mother tongue. I think it is when I first began to defy authority. I think it was at that moment when I knew, there's something wrong.

I stayed in Alberni four years. I didn't know my father had passed away. When I got home my grandfather had gone. There is hatred something awful. My people didn't write, couldn't … it was a long journey. They take me away from the place of my birth and teachings of my Elders. I have a very dear friend who when he came home, there was no communication with his parents. Government almost won their battle of Canadianizing the "savage," as they called us. It says on the legal paper: a child can't communicate with his mom and dad – only in English. There was no communication.[61]

Russell and I had the power and will to hang on through something that I didn't understand at that time, but knew something was going to happen. We never lost our mother tongue. That defying authority at that age came to play in my life very bad. For it is something that the residential school has taught people that resisted against it. My friend went on the same journey, a no-good journey. I think it really bothered his mind. Not long after that, I joined the same path he went. I didn't know that so many of us went in that direction, to hide the pain, hide the shame, and we drowned it in alcohol.

Reggie Wilson: Keeping Us Down Underneath Their Feet

In Alberni a nice guy named Reggie Wilson, called him "Dusty," kind of took me under his wing. He'd done more of teaching me English than any teacher. He was quite a bit older than me; he must have been maybe 17, 16. Anyway, he graduated and asked the principal if he could go to high school. After eight days, they kicked him out of the residential school, Grade 8.[62] I think at that time, if I remember right, the principal of that school was Caldwell. And he heard Reggie's plea that he wanted to continue his education. There's two high schools in two little towns close together, Alberni and Port Alberni. Both little towns had high school and both of them refused. The government said that there's no Indians could be educated. When you think back of what the government done of keeping us down underneath their feet. I look and admire my ladies, all of the Native people across Canada. Maybe one person… don't know, graduated from high school. He didn't understand English well. None of us do.

I tried to put words together to say how proud I am of my little niece, Dr. Jackie Green, high degree in education. In my lifetime of over 80 years, with the flashback to Reggie, I said to my niece, "Dr. Green, a breakthrough. Something's happening."

Four Chiefs: Became Leaders of Our People to Give Them Hope

I was in Port Alberni with Bella Coola's Chief Pootlass. At Alberni his name was Lawrence King. And when he came out he was, like me, a chronic alcoholic. Somewhere along the line something changed, and his grandfather said, "He is changed." He grew into a chief. There was the hereditary chief of Masset, Art Pearson; I was in Port Alberni with him too. And Hereditary Chief Jacob Nyce in Canyon City, Nass River, big chief. All of us were at residential school.[63] I sat down sometimes, I gave them a call and talked to them: "Can you share your story of how you changed your life? How did you correct your life? How did you manage to swim out of that river of alcoholism and make it ashore? Share with me how you done your journey." Every one of us survived. Every one of us had the same story. They almost killed me for talking in my mother tongue. Now it is alive. It is amazing, when I see so many of us – four of us – all suffered in Port Alberni, became leaders of our people to give them hope. The government failed … hearing me talk my language – my mother tongue.

Who Is this Person Torturing Us?

Peter Allan is the name I heard, Mr. Allan.[64] He hurt the boys bad, but wasn't just me – there was a bunch of us. I don't know what year it was, I may have been home maybe five, six years and I stole my grandfather's revolver. I came down to Vancouver Island, went to Alberni but couldn't find Mr. Allan. I was going to shoot him. I met Lawrence King and I told him afterwards what I tried to do. He says: "It's not worth it, Brother. He is not worth it." Going back in the Queen Charlotte Strait, I threw the revolver overboard. Maybe I was blessed not to meet my tormentor, as I was determined to kill him.

Vincent, my little brother, is the only one who ran away from Alberni and they never found him or captured him to bring him back.[65] He ran away with three others from Alberni. The others got caught by the police. He worked for a fisherman towards the end. They found his body under a wharf in the cannery in Port Edward. He was decomposed, no idea who he was, so the Sally Anne [Salvation Army] buried him in an unknown grave in Rupert. That fall my mum said, "Go look for him." Sister Louisa was already in Rupert and married. I stayed in a little hotel.

I met a policeman. Oh, he was a gentleman: "Can I help you, Cecil?"

"Yes," I said. "I think he had partial dental plates but no clue where he had it made."

"That is a good start," the policeman said. So, he went through all the dentists in Rupert, and one morning, came a knock on the door.

"Hey, get dressed," he says. "I think we have broke through something." We went to the dentist.

"Does your brother have a middle name?" dentist asked.

I said "Yes, Vincent Harry Paul."

There was a partial plate that they took from his decomposed body and that is how we found his grave. I phoned Sister Louisa: "I'm going home to tell the family."

I wanted to dig him up and take him home but my auntie Louise [not to be confused with sister Louisa] said: "*Q'uu x*w*enox*w *q'uu.* No, my child, no. Let him be. He suffered too much and too long. Cousin Frances's son was buried in the Prince Rupert cemetery too. He needs family to keep him company." I think Vincent went to Alberni the same time as Mr. Plint was there.[66]

When they took that school down in Alberni, I got one brick. It really bothered me, so I took it outside and put it in the smokehouse. Quite a while afterward, I told a friend about it. He says, "I got one too. I brought a witness from my council and went up the hill and I shot it to pieces."

I says, "I took mine and took it to the middle of the Douglas Channel and throwed it overboard." Who is this person torturing us to do such a thing like that? They didn't understand what has happened to us, eh? That friend had a very difficult time with that Mr. Plint – very bad.

Butedale: Beginning of a Bad Journey

After Alberni Residential School, I went to a little place called Butedale, and I worked in the cannery for a little while.[67] When I first got to Butedale I was 14 years old. It was a segregated place: Indians in one place, Chinese another, white people close to the store. I was in the Indian place. I was fishing, 14 years old. You get a share of the catch, but because I was so young and green, captain gave me a half-share. I was a dishwasher. Then after that I worked in that cannery for quite a number of years. At age 14 I was offered a drink, and I took it. That was the beginning of a bad journey. I became a chronic alcoholic. I got drunk and I never sobered up for well over 30 years. That part of my life was awful.

Frogs: The Indian Way of Teaching

One of my Elders took us out, close to Butedale. He got us into the right position for this canoe, then he took a paddle and hit the side of the canoe. There was this little creek that trickled out to the ocean, and when he banged on the canoe, the little creek got bigger. Everyone was in awe. We thought he was magic, but he is telling us, "I'm not. Okay. Pick your paddles up." We didn't go far, tide was falling, so he told us to anchor the canoe out so we don't have to drag it down. We went for a hike, and we went up to a little lake there. It was summertime and the outfall was just a little trickle. Went by the river. "Walk softly," he said, "and don't make noise." We went to this little lake. Then we make noise, frogs all jump in the water and it made the river come up. The lake was just full of them frogs and little things what we seen.[68] He had to show us that for us to believe. The Indian way of teaching – visual, not behind a desk with a piece of paper and writing and don't know how to spell. Outdoors is our classroom – visual teaching. What a benefit it has done me, our Native way, and that method of teaching of the children of visual teaching. But that has gone now too. Now they are going to classroom, inside eight hours a day; our classroom was open 24 hours a day. Got to be there to see. How he would put it together, that bang would penetrate or echo up to the lake. I just came out from Alberni. I was

14, I guess. I left him later, I drink and never look back. He was my teacher. Too bad I didn't listen, eh?

Baptism of Jail

After leaving Butedale the first time, I got on the Union Steamship Line. I learned later was called *Cardena*, the name of the passenger boat. There were three boats, *Catala* and *Chehalis*. They called it second class. Second-class Indians. We were put way down at the bottom of the boat. We experienced a lot of bad things. I lived in Rupert in the harbour, in summer at fishing time. They had a Canadian Fish Cannery right there, close to Cow Bay. It was what Butedale was too, Canadian Fish Company. I seen a war story movie is on, and I go into see it with Russell Ross. We went into this beautiful theatre, and we sat down and soon an usher came: "You're not supposed to sit here. Over there is where the Indians sit."

I asked, "Do we pay less than those that are entitled for this seat?" And I didn't move. Before the start, two big officers come. They took me away, didn't take my friend. I managed somehow to get in deeper trouble, maybe because I'm not going to move. That was our journey.

I stayed two nights in jail because I didn't want to leave a seat that belong to a different race and go to where the Indians sit. It was a baptism of jails after that; I come to know many in my life. And that jail hurt me more and maybe just as much as what Alberni done. It went beyond the walls of Alberni now. The segregation was outside; as I'm not free, I don't feel free as to where this Indian can move. For my journey for refusing to leave, I stayed two days in the Rupert jail.[69] At times I'd stay awake, thinking how much of my life was behind bars. How much, how long did I stay? It wasn't that young girl's [usher] fault; she was following orders, eh? For a while, I blamed her. Until I learned the little ladies were just following orders. I never did see that war movie; they took me out before the show started. I had a show in the jail cell.

In Rupert every where you go signs say *No Indians* except for the Grand Café, run by a Chinese guy, Mr. Chan. He served everyone there: Chinese, Japanese, Indian. I come in and ask him, "Can I work for you for a meal?" He says, sure, and serves me a T-bone steak. Washed dishes for six hours for that T-bone steak. Always had a pack of cigarettes for me too. My tormentors put up signs that say *No Indians*. They are from far away. Mr. Chan is from far away and invites the Indian in. What is different in the mind of this person, who sees everyone as a human being?[70]

I remember a platform that was going down towards a dock in Prince Rupert, and the place was called Cow Bay. I was going down a ramp and there was a little tap above me, and there was an elevator going up, and from that it was not far that the big ships come, and I was just waking up. During that night somebody opened the water and I was lying in the gutter…lying in water. I felt the vibration where I was lying, and I heard one person say, "Look at that drunken Indian." I heard footsteps disappear and managed to get the strength to get up. Why did them words stay with Wa'xaid? Why did them words stay – "You are a drunken Indian"? Dried myself off, looked for friends to go get drunk again, and hide the shame. I heard the words that I heard, not knowing what it meant. I didn't accept it, I guess, the pain was too thick to penetrate with words like that. I believe I was not sick enough to hear words like that. "Look at that drunken Indian."

I think the worst thing I seen was a young woman, and she was going to school in Lejac Residential School. It is closed. Just this side of Prince George to Vanderhoof. There is a Catholic school there called Lejac, and my wife would come with me when I go to meetings sometimes, and I went to one in Houston and there was a young girl in there who got talking to my wife and they really got along. My wife invited her to go have lunch with her, and she was telling my wife that when she, "first was a lady and first had my period, they took me to the infirmary like a first aid station. Doctors came in, put me to sleep to take my tonsils out." Here they tied her tubes because she was an Indian. Fourteen years old, 15 – whenever the period starts – and she was crying when she tell my wife. "How many grandchildren do you have?" she asks. "I will never hold a child." That woman died sad. I went to her funeral. I cried. I cried for that lady. Longing for a child. Wicked people who do that. Catholic. When I heard that, I thought, what I went through was nothing compared to what that lady went through. How she survived? I admired her courage. Lot of other people get drunk, commit suicide, couldn't cope with what happened. Look at that drunken Indian lying in the gutter. I was there. I was in the gutter. When you mentioned Cow Bay, I try to remember... a bunch of boats there tied up, notice a tap, and I was lying on that thing and somebody put the water over me. I was passed out. Lucky I didn't drown.

I got a teaching from the Kitlope that stuck with me. One day, a killer whale was trying to get back to his house and he gets sucked up by the tide, gets stranded. I was from the Killer Whale Clan. There is a grizzly bear by him and a bunch of wolves also nearby. The grizzly was protecting the killer whale from the wolves. One from the ocean and one is from the land and they trust each other. The grizzly was the protector of the killer whale, and I was from the Killer Whale Clan. The wolf was government, and the grizzly was my protector against the government. I thought about this teaching from the Kitlope, and it changed me inside. It helped me to understand what happened to Wa'xaid. I got all my teachings from the Kitlope.

They Fought So Well for Us

Guy Williams was married to my auntie, my father's sister. He and Dr. Peter Kelly worked together a lot with the Native Brotherhood. He and Guy, on the first trip to Ottawa, they had to use their own money. He told me himself: "Just us paid for that." Think of that, the urge to fight for his people; fought for us to be able to vote. Mothers of babies never received nothing until Guy and Dr. Kelly fought for those things, which other people got. They fought so well for us.[71]

Two people had a vision, and they cut that vision off. Our community could have been self-sufficient with a small hydro-electricity. The government told Heber [Maitland], "You can't put a small dam back there." A second round came with a new leader of the Haisla Nation. Harry Amos [Gerald Amos's father] didn't believe the Indian agent. Harry went up the hill and said, "What do you see? When you have a chance go up above that waterfall on the left-hand side. Take a look at that valley. It is impossible to miss."

I said, "*Wii sii o 'tla.* That means 'go ahead and challenge it.'" That is all I said to my friend. "Challenge the Indian agent, challenge the government, challenge our people if you can't persuade them to put in the hydroelectric." We are going to try again. We could do it. If we could bring the people together and support 100 per cent, we could do it. We could have our own electricity.

Last Canoe

Talking about the last carved canoe, the last one that is Xenaksiala-built, is lying in the graveyard in Kemano. I tell Johnny Wilson, "I'm going to burn it, Brother."

He says, "No. Let's put it into the grave. Let Mother Nature look after it. Don't burn it; it has so much memories. Crab River is how far we go with this canoe to get the clams and the cockles. We go up to the Kitlope with it. We harvest the salmon and the mountain goat. The transportation back and forth to Kitamaat. How many people would it take? Eight. It was a beautiful canoe."

One year I got lucky fishing and bought a little 5½ Evinrude. "John," I says, "let's try it. Okay." I cut the end off a beautiful canoe and spoiled it by putting the 5½ horsepower on there, but I look at him smiling: "No more paddling, John. We are getting modernized.[72] From here to there, what took us a week, we got there in one day. "But now I pay the price, John. I don't get the paddling exercise anymore. 'Round the corner, the deer and bear will run away with our noise. Paddling allowed us near." So, there was good and bad from manual labour to a gas motor. If you ask me which one I like best, I'd say, at that time, the motor. So that is the story of the last Xenaksiala canoe.

Grease Trails: Road for Trading

They had two grease trails for trading the oolichan: one behind Kemano and one from Kitlope River, Xesdu'wäx^w. Because there was a cannery way up there, people used to walk down and work in the cannery. And they'd bring smoked moose meat and mountain goat, and we'd exchange with grease. All the way up over the mountains. Our people call them *Aat'lä'sumx kalas*, road for trading. When the birth of the Native Brotherhood was happening, my grandfather – his name is Johnny Paul – he went all by himself. That river, once you pass a lake and then you go into Xesdu'wäx^w. That river is really swift. That trail begins there, and he walked over to attend the meeting of Native Brotherhood. And he was the last one to walk over that way.[73] All by himself.

Wolf with One Paw

After the fishing season at Butedale, we'd go home and do some trapping and hand logging. See that right there, where my two fingers are missing, and it looks like a little ball? I was about 20. Crosby Smith, my cousin, went with me to the

73

Kitlope to go hunting in the estuary. The geese were maybe 200 yards away. We had our raingear on in the fall time. The tidal grass is flattened down, and when the tide goes out you lay down the same way. I had a good gun. It had a pump action, and my grandfather gave me a little single shotgun when I was a little boy. I loved that gun and I took it. Then in the fall, the tidal grass was kind of slimy, slippery. With my raingear, I went down fast. I had that gun half-cocked so it was safe. It wasn't made like that to not fire, but I told him, "Crosby, run to your left." I lost control of that little gun and it had enough weight and momentum to pull the trigger, and I am trying to push away, and I looked at what happened. Two of my fingers were shot off. I took my toque and covered my hand up and said, "I'm hurt bad, Brother."

From Kitlope to where I live in Kemano, we had a 5½ Evinrude on the canoe. I don't know how many hours it took. I remember I needed water: "Go underneath that waterfall and get me wet. I'm beginning to get tired." I don't remember reaching Kemano, but I woke up asking Crosby for a soft drink. Crosby got up and ran up there, up the highway, and finally stopped someone and they took me up to the first-aid station. Doctor took me with a helicopter to Prince Rupert.[74] Went to this big guy, they say he carried me like a little baby. The only time I remember, they were wheeling me into the hospital. I was in there for nine months. The guy who worked on me was Dr. Mack. He was an air force doctor. He cut my hands to get them like that. He done a beautiful job. I still have movement; that is what I mean by "he did a wonderful job."

I had always had my hand in a pocket. This is the story of how I took it out. My little uncle, my dad's brother, Uncle Charlie Wilson, he gave me a *cˣ uxʷa (Choukwa)* – you call it, a cleansing ceremony. He gathered the people, big chiefs in order: "I want to cleanse my nephew, my son. He had a bad accident. He hurt his right hand almost eight years àgo. I am going to take his hand out for you, Haisla chiefs." He came and took out my hand and he lifted it up and showed it to the Haisla people. "Injured when he was young, and I now watch that he no longer should be ashamed. His new name is *k'uks gˣans dlasiagʷmix*, Wolf with One Paw. Like my nephew, the wolf hid his paw." Wolf came and taught me that you could survive, so that is my other name *k'uks gˣans*. Never had it in my pocket again after that. I tell that story sometimes. After the cleansing ceremony I was all right, 30 years as longshoreman.

Cumshewa

We were in big Davis rafts in Aero in Cumshewa Inlet with my friend, Art Pearson; there were three Pearson brothers from Queen Charlottes that I met up in Alberni.[75] They cabled together big bundles in the boom. It was after the war. That was where I met my friend, the Frenchman, Albert Jacobs. I worked with him almost 30 years at Kitimat. He was a crane operator, big crane. Before that, he was an operator on Davis rafts at Cumshewa. I remember my superintendent, Panicky Bell.[76] He fired me three times: "Don't let that ever happen again! Go on, get out of here! Go to work!"

I Went Fishing Instead

Then there is the time I worked with the surveyors when they built that highway.[77] They hired Albert Walker, Bill Starr and I. This was the river that changed. This was our base here. We brought the material up to the surveyors. They rented a canoe from Jimmy Henry, and I was in a canoe with Bill Starr. Bill had been in the war in Korea and just come home. Albert had a homemade riverboat. Two boats. We go all the way up to the Kitimat bridge. We go to Terrace. That was our base camp there for the surveyors. We got caught in a flood, so Bill and I walked out to get help and food to Lakelse where there was an old dirt road to Terrace. We got to Terrace and got drunk and forgot about the hungry camp. Then we remembered when we sobered up. Had to fly in an airdrop while we were hungover.

I am the only one alive now. Bill left first and then Albert.

August, we came down here and I met Crosby Smith. He asks me, "I am one man short to operate a drum on the seine boat."

I says, "I got a job."

He says, "What do you think I am offering? It is in your blood..." He says, "...fish. Oceans in your blood, not the river."

He persuaded me. I went up, told the boss I was going to go fishing, He said, "I want you boys to consider coming with us on our next one in the Amazon River. We'll need two operators." I went fishing instead. Crazy.

I met one Amazon Native person when Ecotrust Canada, Ian Gill, gave me that award, and this big chief gave me a big fish scale.[78] Gee, it was beautiful. He said you could wear it in ceremony. He says you could wear it any time you want. It had a red thing in the middle. They told me what it was, some kind of a jewel in the middle. Real pretty rock. Didn't know the history of it. Didn't know why I got it. I met the big chief. I still regret today that I went fishing; I could have seen the Amazon.

There I Met a Beautiful Girl

While I was fishing, that was when I met Cecelia's mom, Marguerite, at Butedale.[79] That was an awful journey. Worked year-round in Butedale Cannery, cold storage there. Halibut fishing was year-round. Not like it is now; you got a quota. None of our people worked in the cold storage. And I worked there for a while. And I worked in that reduction plant, preparing for the herring fishing. My first experience with segregation was our home plant, Butedale. We went by there the other day, you and me. When you experience something bad and somehow you think you'll heal, you cross where the dagger is put in your heart. I thought it was healed, I thought it would go, but each time I pass this place, it will hurt.

There I met a beautiful girl. Oh, she was beautiful. It was the second-most damaging part of my life concerning the colour of my skin, as an Indian. This young girl I fell in love with, she was not Indian. Marguerite's parents were both in the air force, and they homesteaded across from Butedale. I come, and ask Marguerite, "Can you walk with me?" And she never left her parents' side, and I walked away. Remember the theatre I talked about? Indians sit over there? I bleed inside for a long time.

We defied authority again in my life – a second time – that was really bad. When I defied authority and went underground, my journey again, has begun. Sneaking, I call it. My little girl-friend and I snuck around together, and they knew, there were eyes all over. Talked with the manager of the place, his name was Bill Malcolm, caretaker of the cannery where I worked. I was called in: "You have to leave." I had to go. It was in the month of October, and a boat was coming in the next day and I had to be on it. And Alcan had started, and they had vessels going into Kemano, and I know the boat was going to go there, the one I was on. I didn't go back to work; I went home. My brother Dan couldn't get a job too. And he says, "What are you going to do, Brother?"

I says, "I'm going to go home and trap for this winter. Springtime, we'll go looking for a job." Gee, that went well, trapping, he and I. My mum had a house here. We came out after New Year's and I told her, "I'm going to go. I'll be back in five years." Brother and I took off. Went to Rupert, sold half of our fur. Went to Vancouver. Auctioned it off. Got a lot of money. That was when my drinking really started. I didn't tell my mum why I left Butedale until when I came back after five years. I made her promise: "Don't you tell anybody. Just you and me know that you have a granddaughter, five years old now, and we don't know where she is."

Eagle Chick

I showed you that eagle's nest coming down the Kitlope, just before you touch the salt water; do you remember that? That nest has been there since my mum was a little girl. Once the north wind came and they found a little eagle chick on the ground, and she took her earring and she put it around the talon of the eagle. The grandfather went and put the chick back on the nest with the earring on there. Few years later, my mum seen this eagle and she seen the earring glitter. That eagle came back, reproduced. It was the one that Grandfather had put that thing on. My mum said, "My granddaughter flew away from my nest … and she's going to come back the way that little one came back to her nest … to reproduce. We're going to see my granddaughter."[80] And we kept that our secret all along. And I didn't know where my grief was. And then I drank some more, and I drank and I drank.

"A daughter that flew away long ago." Eagle on stump at Misk'usa, 2017.
MAPLE LEAF ADVENTURES

That child was put up for adoption to a minister in the United Church. He was just ordained, and they sent him to an Indian reserve outside Rupert called Port Simpson. I have a little younger sister, Louisa, that got married to a Tsimshian, Murray Smith, and that was where their home was when this new minister came. The young people befriended them, John and Sharon Cashore.[81] After Cecelia was adopted, Sharon gave birth to twin boys. Murray would play with Cecelia while my sister helped Sharon with the twins. They didn't know Cecelia was her niece. How many years, I don't know.

Tulsequah: Getting the Shame Out of Us

That's when I went north after that. I worked in Tulsequah Mine.[82] We had to go to Juneau. That is where the boundary line is, Canadian. I worked in the mine there with the Belgian wrestler; met him in the streets. Both broken. I lied when I said I worked on the mine; I worked in rock drilling but not a mine. The first cheque was $23 dollars; it gave me a tin of tobacco and rain gear. It's going to last me for three days, and we put $5 in, me and this Belgian wrestler, got in a blackjack game, my goodness we won. We won! Ah! $4,800. We split that. I think we quit, went to Juneau and spent one week in Juneau, then we got deported to Ketchikan, both broke. That was part of the healing, getting the shame out of us.

Kay Boas: They Gave Him a Chance

I met the Oxford Group[83] way before I returned to my little granny teaching me about the Great Spirit. Oxford Group, it

Cousins (unbeknownst to anyone), Port Simpson, Lax Kw'alaams, 1964. Left to right: Susan Smith, Cecelia Cashore, Tom Smith.
CASHORE FAMILY

Gerald Amos, John Cashore, Louisa Smith, Cecil Paul, Kitlope, 1993.
SPENCER B. BEEBE, ECOTRUST

was a teaching of Christianity and spirituality. You read the book, and they call it the bible. That's why they sent someone around the coast to teaching Oxford Group and Christianity. As I understand it, Ebby T. went to the Oxford Group and took it to the AA [Alcoholic Anonymous]. That was with Bill W. Ebby, was the one rescued from jail by Oxford Group who were Christian people. They were going to throw the key away of the jail. His mind was pickled, and the young men gave him a chance with Your Honour: "We'll see what we can do." And the judge had compassion. I remember thinking, "Is anyone still a member of the Oxford Group?" We were on a boat somewhere with Kay Boas.[84] She was Oxford Group.

When I First Came Back

When I first came back to Kitamaat, I sat with the three hereditary chiefs to try and learn Haisla ways. I was told that there was an oolichan camp down one of the small tributaries of the Kitimat River. There was a small village and even a field. One of the Haisla Elders, Samson Ross, at oolichan time of year, would come long after they stopped coming here and sit here, and I asked him, "Why?"

He tell me, "I can still hear the sounds of the river, the laughter and the oolichan. So I come here to remember." Now the laughter has been killed, like the oolichan. They raped this valley. Two nations, Haisla and Xenaksiala, were the richest in the country with five rivers with oolichan in them. I have witnessed the death of a river.

Going up to Terrace, you'll see William's Creek. My wife's

grandfather's, that is her family trapline. And he had a place close to Hartley Bay, where they dig clams. That is his territory too. Fin Island. Mae, my wife, was a big daughter of a big chief.[85] And I lived... when I think about my little grandson, he's actually going to live in my footprint. But when I met her, I was a chronic alcoholic. I stopped drinkin' a little bit, but I couldn't quit completely. Made bad things. Made bad decisions. And finally, we stayed together. Four children came into the world under Williams. Not Paul because we was just living together. When the last one came, Cecil Junior, she says, "Let's get married and give him your name."

I says, "Okay." Went to her father. Proposed to her.

He looked at me, he says, "No, my brother will give you away. My brother Fred."

We went to her aunt, her uncle, and they say, "Okay."

We got married with only a few friends. When I fully changed my life and seen different things, I look at her father, and the woman that I love and of how I treated her. Here is this big chief of the Haisla, dreaming that he'd walk down the aisle with his oldest daughter. And this drunk denied him that. I denied him. I hurt this good man. When he was dying of cancer, I went up to him and I apologized for what I'd done and what I see now. When I got through apologizing of why I'd thought he'd asked his brother to give his daughter away – too ashamed to give a beautiful daughter to a drunken man like me. And when I finished (I had all the children go out), he said, "You let the children in now, my son." He'd never called me that before, "my son." Was that his way of saying: "I forgive you"?

Beaver Story: You're Bragging Too Much

One day, my wife said, "Dad is coming in. He looks mad." I called my uncle – my dad – Charlie Wilson.[86] She says, "Oh, put the tea on, he'll get happy."

"Do you want some tea, Dad?" I ask him in my language. "*Lukala*?" It means "are you hurting inside?" "What is the matter?" And he got right to the topic of what he came in for.

"Yes, I am," he said. "After we're finished oolichan fishing, I want you to go see two of your brothers, Samuel and your brother Dan." My wife poured him a cup of tea; I had coffee. And he says, "Why I say this, is that I feel myself getting weak, and I haven't showed you kids our tribal territory in the Kitlope, the names of the different places. We'll be up there for two months."

Gee, I was excited. He had me worried when he said, "I'm getting weak; I won't be able to walk far." The next day, I gathered my two brothers. Called 'em for supper and told 'em what our dad said, and amazed that they both agreed.

We left Kemano. We stop here, stop there, him telling us our names. White man name, our name all the way up. Went to Matthews Bay, Kowesas. He told us the name of the chief that owns it, then the first little river when you're going to Kemano, on the chart, it is called Wolf Creek. "We're going to trap and shoot beaver," he says, "to pay for my gas," while he's teaching us our tribal territory.

Everybody put their catch in Kowesas that night – our first hunting as the four of us. I was the only one that got a beaver, a beautiful medium-sized beaver. And I bragged to my younger brother Dan and the one younger-than-me brother Sam what a good shot I was. "What are you guys doing?" I says.

Next day, we had to travel, and my uncle took me away from my two brothers: "*Mii'ła suu x^wenox^w*. You are wrong, my son. You are bragging too much to your brothers. Do you think you are way up there? Such a good shot? Got to correct yourself." I never bragged to anyone again. After that month and a half, we got to the pool where I was born. The main camp house was still there. "*Gin tsaquai'lii*. How much did you get? We got 52 pelts. Did you hear what I was saying about bragging? Out of that 52, only the first one you got – no more – and the rest were all caught by the others." What a beautiful teaching. It didn't hurt me. He noticed every action; he watched his nephews.

The Goose Story: Only Take One

We started out at Kowesas. We walk up the river. There was a triangle of small little trees, almost like a house. Dad [Charlie Wilson] tell us this history, and I heard it from Sam Hall too, that they see that thing [prospecting survey mark] sitting on the banks of the river. Americans finding gold up at Kowesas, and every one of them died. They just figured someone mentioned gold. Only one miner left after they killed one another. Someone else must have told another person, and that guy went and killed him too. I often think it might have been Knutson.[87] Do you know about Knutson? He used to live in Butedale. I met Knutson up there when I was young boy and up in Kemano. How did one man winter there? Because it used to freeze up, and he stayed in Kowesas all winter long.

Something about Knutson baffles me. Was he a Swede? Tough old guy. He was a prospector.

Anyway, when we got to Kowesas where the geese make their nests in the stumps along the river. Grandfather had once told Dad [Charlie] and his brother, "Only take one." He knew that the geese only produce two eggs, and he told the boys, "Take one." But no, they didn't listen. They take two eggs and the geese – Mom and Dad – attacked Dad and his brother. Grandfather came to them and asked, "How many did you take from that one nest?"

Dad says, "Two from that nest."

Grandfather says, "Go take it back right now. Go take it back." His voice was commanding, eh? Not right with these boys disobeying his teaching. His voice comes up: "When you take the one egg back the geese will settle down." They did. After that I never eat eggs. That was the first egg I had in a long time. That is why I held it. I think of that memory.

Mountain Goats: He Was Calling Home

That same trip, my two brothers and I were all skinning beaver. Someone say, "Hey, look at all the mountain goats up there!"[88] We all stopped and look.

Yeah, there were nine mountain goats in the opening, and our teacher Uncle Charlie says, "*Yä'ga'lum ɫloos gaida nox*ʷ*aid noox*ʷ *k'aɫid.*" He says, "Look! That's what you're going to use when you cook a feast up for me when I go to sleep." After he said that, everybody start skinning again. That story stayed with me, what he said.

I don't know how many years later – quite a few years – I called my two brothers back. My uncle Charlie was very sick then; he was in the hospital. I go and see him, and he was in the spirit world already. He reaches up, picks something, and he's chewing in his mouth. I ask, "*Ma'sii hum siks Dii?* What are you eating, Dad?"

He asked, "Don't you see? Don't you see all the berries?" He tells me we're up in the Kitlope. I sat with him for a couple of hours and then I left, and I called my two brothers.

"I think we should go get four mountain goats to prepare for his feast, for when he dies." Dan was working. Samuel didn't answer. So my good friend, Johnny, Johnny Wilson, came.

I phoned Sister Louisa. Her boy Tom was strong; he was a big man. He says, "I'll go with you, Uncle."

My uncle Charlie had a trapline about halfway from here to Kemano called Geltuis – means long inlet – and we see a lot of mountain goats up high, but this must have been in November. The fog came down, and the teaching of what I'm trying to get at reminds me of the *T'ismista*, the hunter that didn't listen.[89] We didn't go up the mountain. The tide was high, so high I put my boat underneath an overhanging branch and took a few branches so we could see out. Just when we were settled there, I opened one Thermos, and we were gonna have a coffee and Pow!…a shotgun noise. Nobody else but him and I.

My nephew look at me. I said, "I think we should go back. This is your grandpa's trapline. He's sending me a message, and I don't know what it is."

Went back to the boat and Johnny was there, and he says,

"I think you guys should take off now. I'll follow. Stay on the shoreline. If you break down if it is too rough, get in the little harbour and come out to meet me."

So we took off in my little boat. When I heard that shotgun, I asked, "What time did we hear that?"

Tom says, "10 after 10, Uncle, in the morning."

We got to Kitamaat, just before dark – 3:30, 4 o'clock in the afternoon. Kitamaat at 10 o'clock they brought Charlie into the church for the funeral service. That's when we heard that shot. That was communication with my uncle to me – he was calling home. But we missed his funeral.

I Could Make Man and Machinery Work in Harmony

We had worked in the booms with a Frenchman, Albert Jacobs, in the Queen Charlottes. He was operator. I worked here in Kitimat, and our boss said they were going to leave pretty soon. "Albert, you can come if you want, and you too Cecil. Our next contract is in River's Inlet." But it was across the bay in Kitimat that they were starting a new boom. "Tomorrow, Albert's going to take half a day off and go apply for the job. Next day you go." Oh, we both got on.

I used to bring all the logs from Kemano. My job was a boom man.[90] They towed all the way, hundred ton. They got it in a big boom. Put onto big trucks. I was a lead hand for I don't know how many years in the boom. The supervisor had to leave, and they asked if I could be a supervisor. They brought me to the head office. I told them, I could work with man and machinery but the other part, like what you do on writing, I couldn't do that. I had to decline to be the supervisor. Didn't go to school, but I could make man and machinery work in harmony.

I never experienced where they logged. I worked in the finishing part where they made paper. And my job was to fill the boats, come in and I load them up with pulp. They go all over the world. The Russians were really friendly. I was on the docks for 30 years. I don't know where that gift I got from Eurocan / West Fraser when I retired went – 31 years.

West Fraser are the ones that had the tree-farm licence for the Kitlope. That's why when I seen those survey markers I talk to my wife. I said, "I might get fired if I fight for this. I am working for the one that has got such tree-farm licence."

We talk for a while, and then she look at me and say, "I'll walk with you. Go ahead and fight for what you believe in." That came from the woman, from Mamie. That what makes me decide: Okay. The journey I have in the Kitlope decided by a woman that has said "I'll walk with you."

Crab River: Is this My Mountain?

One hundred and fifty years ago, there was war amongst my people.[91] They were raided for food and grease. The raiders slaughtered a young warrior's family, so he went for revenge. This young man couldn't believe that he survived what he went to do. It was a moonlit night, and he stopped the canoe and the canoe drifted alone. In the middle of the river, he stopped paddling and he looked, and he said, "Is this my mountain? Or am I dreaming?"

And then he heard the quietness of the evening and that little stream coming down. "You are home, my child. You are in *Xesdu'wäx*ʷ [Huchsduwachsdu]." And it is the first time he heard his homeland talk to him through the sounds of the river. He listened to the waterfall across the bay and this creek here. He could hear it all welcoming him back, and the breeze that you feel.

"Warm breeze," he said, "blows on my face. I am home, home to my mountain and I am alive."

Healing Journey

1971–1994

Salmonberry and Riceroot:
A Gift of the New Season

Anyway, there was a journey of loneliness and stuff, and I wasn't well and I'm getting more sick with this disease of alcoholism. I try to remember the hell I was in then. I don't know if you've experienced loneliness. I knew I was sick, but I never knew where it come from. I didn't know where this illness started; I didn't know how to attack it. The thought of suicide, I remember this too, July. I remember this trip, when I go up there, somehow my drinking stopped a little bit, and I knew that something in the Kitlope – in my heart – was something there, and I go.

It was July 18, 1971. I was drifting down the river, a warm breeze would hit me, the next second it would be cold. I stopped my paddling and I drifted there. It was a breath of my Creator. I went to where I was born, and I pulled the canoe up and laid down and the words was coming: "You're in bondage; you're a prisoner." I got up and I walked around to where I remember having coffee with my dad, my granny, and this word keeps coming up: "You're in bondage to your drinking." This is now beginning to register, and I told this pickled mind that I'm here on a healing journey and the memory of my grandmother. And then the things she asked me, "What was it like in the nine years, what you remember in the Kitlope?" All the beautiful teachers, the peace I remember I had in my heart.

That memory of my little granny saying, *"Mä s'i sax ga süüs?* What do you want? What are you here for?" And I'm talking to her memory. I'm going crazy, I thought. And I sat down and

Salmonberry flower, "a gift of the new season," Kitlope River.

told her of my journey, and the memories of her kept floating in this mind. After little Granny told me the story of that, I went to the estuary, and there's a flower, the salmonberry.[92] I walked around.

She came to me and said, "Son, this one little flower in middle of June, it become a berry. When you take it and put it in your mouth it's sweet. It's a sugary taste." In the estuary there's a purple flower. I dug it up and she showed me the root of it. Here it was white as rice. Two flowers: the first one the Great Spirit gives us as a gift of the new season to feed our bodies; it's the spring, the salmonberry sugar. This one here's the wild riceroot. He feeds us under the ground. We take them and we combine it with the oolichan grease and we eat it together – *aiis'dllams a'sinx* – a new season the Creator has given us. All these teachings, our spirituality drowned out through all 40 years of trying to hide the pain. Hide the shame. Until I'd had enough … and I went home to the Kitlope.

I would go, especially at midnight when everything is quiet, around the lake. The four villages were guardians: the killer whale, beaver, eagle and raven [or five with salmon]. My grandmother tells me that they invite each other, and they laugh and they dance. I'm in this middle of the river and I'm the opposite – I'm not laughing, I'm not dancing. Why is that so? A quiet moment. It's so loud sometimes – stillness, opposite from how I feel. I think when I say these things that I crave so much about in my journey, since I managed to put the alcohol away was a touch of serenity, peace within.

Each journey I take I feel it will improve: the feeling of

Riceroot flower, "a gift of the new season,"
Kitlope estuary, May 2015.
GREG SHEA, MAPLE LEAF ADVENTURES

beauty, my eyes, my vision is clearing from alcohol, the sweat was almost pure, there was no poison coming out from my body, and I bathe in the artery of Mother Earth, cleansing me in a lake.

It was that one evening, as I was drifting down to where I was born and at my main camp, I sat there. I said, "Great Spirit, thank you for this land. Help me find myself, Great Spirit. Who am I? What is it you put before me? What is the destination of my life? Who am I?" I got in my boat, just before dark went back into the lake. I stayed there for two days.

I think now, when I look back, I think it was fasting because I had nothing to eat. I just reached over the side of my canoe and I drank the beautiful river water. I come out of there that day, for a moment during the evening, I was one with the universe, everything was fine, but I swear it didn't last more than a second. I had a touch of serenity in the Kitlope. I go back, I tell my wife what happened. I had the strangest experience, something came over me, and made me feel good.

When I look back on it, there was not a breath of wind, nothing, quiet. But something inside exploded. I remember I laughed out loud. I heard the echo; I'm not alone on this lake. I think the Great Spirit penetrated something, opened my eyes a little bit. I told Gerald that: him and I go. When you come to the Kitlope, I tell you, you can not help but change when you leave. You change your thought; you change your feeling. I said, "It's a cathedral, Gerald. I think that's what changes."

He says, "Is only the lake the cathedral?"

Flowers in the Kitlope River estuary, 2015.
GREG SHEA, MAPLE LEAF ADVENTURES

I said, "I don't think so. I think the whole valley is a cathedral."

I began to sense that there's something here in the Kitlope. I could break the cycles of the life I'm going through, an ugly life. I called the journey a healing journey. My wife would say, "Where are you going?"

I'd say, "If I don't come back in ten days, I'll be up in the Kitlope."

She was saying, "You're on your healing journey?"

I'd say, "Yes."

She'd prepare things for me to go. She sensed a change, somebody had seen the change. She was a beautiful lady. Her father accepted me for who I was – "You could have my daughter."[93]

Wii sii o 'tla: Don't Be Afraid to Speak

They had an election with the young lady Iona Campagnolo.[94] She was completely for the Eurocan expansion. She said that the water would be so good that you could drink a glass of fresh water after the expansion. I said, "Your Honour, let me have the honour of giving you the first glass of that water." Now there is no oolichans on the Kitimat. How far does the poison go into the riverbanks? How deep does it go? How many years will it take to purify the artery of the Mother Earth? They took away from us something so precious to our culture.

That day one of the Elders comes up to me and says, "*Wii sii o 'tla*. Don't be afraid to speak." He was telling me to have the courage to keep speaking out. They listened to industry before the Indian, and now Kitimat is still polluted. The almighty dollar.

The Largest Tree in Kitimat

Kitimat town council, they decide to dedicate a park to the biggest Sitka spruce left there.[95] Sisi Kaas. It is still alive, eh? The pitch is coming down Hyda wakalla off this tree. This old tree is going back to Mother Earth. Just like humans going back to the womb of Mother Earth slowly. Pretty soon it will fall back to dust, the largest tree in Kitimat. We appreciate the beauty of Mother Earth. In many ways, if you slow down in our journey, appreciate this wilderness, stop for a moment in your fast life and relax a little bit – you see how big it is? How the north wind blows over a hundred miles an hour? All the weight…just imagine how far these roots go all over to keep it up. This root here is beginning to decay…look at how big it is. How far does it go? It has one root in the middle; that is the one that feeds it with water. That root is broken and the tree falls. Any tree will die just with that one artery breaking that will drink water. Twisted and entwined. The north wind blows well over and yet it stays.

Gerald, he got invited to when they were opening the big tree park. Gerald was the chief councillor, Kitamaat Village, and Kitimat Mayor Joanne Monaghan was a big one here. Gerald said, "I didn't go, even though I was invited." He said, "Used to be hundreds of them trees like that. They raped our land. How many houses could that big tree build? And not a penny came to our village. I am not accepting this invitation."

I said, "Good for you." He thought I was going to argue and tell him to go.

Virgil: The Man that Broke the Arrow

One day I'm working – I'm sober maybe eight years – and a guy came up to me. He said, "How you stop drinkin', Indian?"

I said, "If you wanna stop, I'll take you to a place that helps us."

He says, "I wanna try."

"Okay. I'll pick you up tomorrow."

As Virgil walked away, every bit of my life was Virgil. He was shaken this way, snot almost down to his knees, staggering. Walked away, and in my mouth, he says, "Brother, I love you. You walk in my moccasins. I love you, my brother."

Virgil was a white man, and he come ask an Indian, "How'd ya stop?" Virgil broke my hatred of the white man. I don't hate. It was the system, not the people. That's what I needed to learn, how to forgive the white man. To trust how to come back. But it's there, because of my little granny. First one salmonberry in June. I'll go to the estuary and pick up some wild rice. Put them together. Thanks, Great Spirit.

Virgil stayed sober for five years; he became my brother. Next thing he says, "I'm well enough go stay close to my family in Vancouver Island." He got a job in Port McNeil.

One wintertime in January, I got a call: "Are you Cecil Paul? We found this thing [card] on a human body, the only one in the wallet, the name on it was you. Are you Cecil Paul?"

"Describe him," I said. "If it is my friend, he got family there."

Who's Virgil? He's telling me through that little piece of paper – the only name he had in his wallet – Cecil Paul and my phone number: "Don't try what I done, or you'll end up like what I did." He's one step ahead of me. He never left me, he's just giving me the courage never to take it with me. "Face the music," Virgil told me. See the way he broke the hatred and mistrust there.

I'd like to go back to this man that broke the arrow, Virgil. I dreamed of dry-out centres and all that, but there's not enough in there to try and put a sick person into society. I think there's more that could be done.[96] When I look back at where I came from, from the gutter, and to where I am today, anyone I see, whether it be an Indian or a white man, or a black man, I will reach out my hand: come with me on my journey. It's much better where we are today because I was there, I know what it feels like. I've been in hell, and now I have a touch of serenity and I wait for my people. I dream, I could raise hell tomorrow. So that's my learning, how to forgive.

Sometime we have a picnic on the river with AA. If you walk slowly you look at this sword fern and it has a stem and every one of them leaves has the same distance. The stem of it is the centre focus. You take one leaf off and you can see it start to lean to one side. Two leaves off, lean more, and then you go all the way to the top and that is the end. That is how life is as an alcoholic. My life was not in centre focus. I lost leaves, I lost my Great Spirit, so I used the fern at the AA meetings. Walk softly when you walk around the bush to look at this artwork. How beautiful it is, and all that beauty was erased from my mind with alcohol. I try to share my experiences of what I see and what I lost all those years. But it came back when I think about my little granny's teachings.

I went to Vancouver, Prince George, Whitehorse, Winnipeg, Prince Rupert – Indigenous meetings all over the place. This guy, I travelled with him for a while, and he asked me to be a speaker at their round-up. There was a few people from Old Crow, and they invited me over there. It was awesome, see no roads or nothing up there. We went in by boat from plane. Lots of sick people there. Maybe 50 years since the Medical Association recognized alcohol as a disease, like cancer, can be cured. Majority of them, in the gutter like I was, manage to crawl out of it. I tried to share my experience of how I got sober, and it was all through going back to the teachings of my little grandmother; and that is what the government wanted, was to take away our language and our culture.

Two times I got invited in Vancouver to the Indigenous AA rally. There was a lot of non-Native people there. Saved my life. This May, the round-up in Kitimat, which I have to prepare for, things were a little hard this year. Too many layoffs at work. Forty bucks usually bought a big meal, all free coffee and food. But that is hard to come by for anyone on social assistance. We talked to cut the cost way down.

I talk about my life but don't realize what I done or said. Brian Falconer was telling when he was going across from Vancouver to Nanaimo, and he sees an Indian kid, Chris Cook,[97] and somehow Brian asked him, "Do you know Cecil Paul over there?"

He says, "He saved my life."

I was invited to talk in Port Hardy Indigenous AA meeting, and I see that guy, Chris Cook, standing around and he asked me, "What are you doing?"

I said, "I'm going to a meeting because I was a drunk."

I made maybe five steps when he said, "Sir, can I come with you?" I stopped, and he still hasn't drunk till this day. Chris Cook.

Kemano Completion Project:
What Damage Is Going to Come of It?

Up here in Kemano River, ten miles south, is a hole Alcan made in the mountain where there is about ten miles of tunnel, and it has a drop of 2,600 feet, and that is where all the turbines are to make electricity.[98] On the other side is a new lake. It made a lot of people happy...a lot of my people happy. All the bread and clothing for people coming from all over the world. It has done a little bit for some people. I was really interested to go and see where the lake is. I went to go visit the Cheslatta people – my mother's people – took me in their rowboat. They told me, "They didn't give us enough time, and then they flooded the whole thing – families, the villages. Not only the Native people, the non-Native people too."

People from the Fraser River, Native and non-Native people, farmers, ask, "Why were we silent on the Kemano 2 completion?" All the hereditary chiefs were concerned, but I didn't know nothing about it except for the goodness of some people who told me about it. For the impact of what they were going to do with Kemano 2 completion was build another dam and send that dam and another big tunnel to come through the mountain that will raise the river. It would destroy a lot of the valley and the Fraser Valley, but what is going to happen to that outcome of where the water's going to come out after the detour? What damage is going to come of it?

I ask the advice of my people, and we send a delegation of a few young people. They went to the community where they were going to dam it and listen to their concerns.[99] What they came back with was some very troubling things. We write down these little things, like oolichan, bear, sea life, eagles and where the project has left nothing; the uncertainty of this valley; the uncertainty of what is going to happen when industry comes and changes something what the Creator has left for us. Will there be no more oolichan? What damage will be done when the river will be raised two feet higher than what it is now? And that is what Alcan tells us. It took eight years for the Kemano oolichan to go back up again.[100] The chiefs decided that we would build a totem pole, and we will use it as a thing for opposing Kemano 2 completion. And when Kemano 2 was finished, we hired a carver. We had it laid in state and we brought it up.

Five Rivers of Oolichan

Five rivers of oolichan: two for the Haisla, which are both contaminated, Kitimat and Kildala; and three for the Xenaksiala: Kemano, Kitlope and Kowesas. Jimmy Henry built the last boiler at Kemano. I got one out of aluminum now. The oolichan don't like flooding water. We see the oolichan not do too well with big spring flood, so when Kemano flooded the river, it washed the oolichan away. They aren't strong swimmers. We were beaver hunting, and we noticed the water rises a few inches and then we know Alcan opened the floodgates. The trapline of the Kemano ran up ten miles and 40 traps or more. I could do it in a day. Now it is a road to the turbines. We asked Alcan to stop raising the waters during their breeding season, March to May, and then had to ask for longer to leave the fry longer to survive.

It took eight years for the Kemano oolichan to go back up the river, but they came back abundant. Even without oolichan, my son and his brother-in-law were the only ones to go up there, waiting in the rain every year. One day they will come back. Patience paid off.[101]

Three generations of the Paul family at
their Kemano oolichan camp.

Cecil Paul testing the oolichan fishery at
the Kemano River, March 2008.

CECIL PAUL JR.

Billy Hall and the *Bekʷus*

In Misk'uk'w is a big valley, and the guy's name is Billy Hall. This is a true story.[102] It is not a child's story. Our people keep saying that they didn't realize that there was hunger in the 1930s. They had an abundance of food: the moose, the deer, the fish. Anyway, Billy went up hunting here with his friend in the place where it divides into two valleys – one this way and one that way. Billy went to the right and his partner went to the left. And when they come to this place, they had one stick. "If that stick is still standing, I am still up, but if I go down before you, I will lay that stick down." That is how they can tell when they come back. Billy went up just before dark, and he seen a black bear. And he had one of them guns that you muzzle loaded, and he went, and he shot this animal. It was a *bekʷus*. And he knew he had made a mistake.

It was a long story, but when he ran down, *bekʷus* were chasing him. He made it down here. He never thought about putting down that stick. He was so scared. And here was his partner waiting for it, and he hauled out. They seen the big things right behind them. He went to Kemano and when he got there, he went to sleep. This is what amazes me, of how my people kept him alive. For one year he slept. How did his system work for one year without waking up? What did they use to feed him? They put bull kelp down his throat to feed him, and when he woke up, he had supernatural powers. He sees things that you and me could never see. He sees a death before it happens. There was this charcoal that he walked across and never got burnt.

In the wintertime, they were having dance and people celebrating a good harvest of salmon. Their cellars were full of food for the winter. And they were dancing. He hollered, and he asked three young men to pick up salmonberry bush. The bush were already asleep; there were no leaves from them. This was in January, and they came and they gave it to him and he looked at it. And there was a fire in the middle of that place and they start dancing around chanting. They went 'round three times. Now there is three salmonberry bushes coming to life. Once more and there was little flower, once more and berries. He went to the highest of chiefs and he said, "What is it?" The salmonberry that he made great. Maybe he touched the Creator. Some power came, like those places in Africa where they go through the fire without getting burned. If my people hadn't experienced that, I wouldn't have believed what I hear. For this mind to conquer fear, conquer heat and to make the salmonberry ripe in the middle of the winter. His tombstone is at home. His grandson was Kenny Hall, who fought for the Kitlope with us. The name for the valley is Misk'uk'w. Place of my birth is Misk'usa. I don't know where the "mis" comes from.

Eighty per cent Industry, 20 per cent Natural Causes

In my journey, I met a friend. His name was Jean-Louis LeMay.[103] He went to visit Kitimat, maybe one or two times, but Jean he was a big guy in Alcan, and his office was in Toronto. When he came here, he told me, "Cecil, I want to come and see what you guys are doing."

I says, "Jean, you know I welcome you, but my government, how would they feel? We are opposing you, my friend. We are opposing you."

Jean says, "But I want to learn. I will strip my title and come as a friend."

Okay, I go to my government and I asked for five minutes when my government had a meeting and I gave the message of my friend. And they asked me to repeat the last words: "He will strip his title and come as a friend." So my government said, "Try to get your friend. How can we penetrate Alcan? How can we deny someone that wants to come as a friend?" So my government said, "Welcome." So I told him to come and he came.

"Jean," I said, "my argument was for years that 80 per cent damage to the Kemano River was caused by your industry, 20 per cent by natural causes."

He says, "Cecil, no, 20 per cent by industry, 80 per cent by natural causes." Naturally there was some conflict there. The outcome was beautiful. They took part when I showed them a lot of things. I videoed the movement of gravel. I talk about what Kemano project was, what it meant for us. I talk about the pollution of the Great Lakes, the oil spill in Alaska.

One day I got a call. Jean said, "I looked through your videos, Cecil. Eighty per cent industry, 20 per cent natural causes."

And I went to my people and I say, "Industry is beginning to change, beginning to listen. Listen to my friend who has stripped his title of this big organization. What can we do to help? I will show you graveyards here in Kemano. A graveyard that was eroded bad by Alcan's boats." I brought my friend to see. He had to see with his eyes what I was trying to say.

Alcan have a big ferry boat, the *Nechako*, that makes big waves. We were trying to make an agreement with Alcan to slow down the boat mid-channel because the waves are so big, and that wave would bounce back off the other shoreline. One day, Jean came up. Never told me, never phoned me. He just said, "Let's go up to Kemano. Bring your friend." I brought Gerald along. We came in unannounced and put the boat around the back out of sight so there was no evidence that there was anyone in the village. Then we wait for the ferry boat to come. The water would hit the other shore and took 20 minutes to come back and giving it a double wave.

"Jean, you want to wait 20 minutes for that second wave to come." Timed it. "How many times does this come a week, Jean?"

He agrees. "Yes, Cecil it is 80 per cent industry, 20 per cent natural causes. What can we do to stop the erosion?"

Jean got on the phone to his men – they must have recognized his voice – and he told them, "Get on your boat and come to the Indian village." We all watched the boat come in. They didn't know we were observing them. They come full blast and Jean witnessed them. I met the young man who was in charge of the boat. The surprise that he had when he met the big chief of Alcan. I brought the young man to show him the erosion. They talked about all the rock that came from that tunnel. Estimated how much it will cost to truck it down, put it on a barge and what machinery we use and then we will make this breakwater. That was the gift from Jean-Louis LeMay.

The breakwater was finished in November. I asked my people, "What are we going to say to Alcan? How can we put it into words to say thank you for saving our graveyard?" The totem pole was the gift. It is called Nanakila, which in my language means the sentry or watchman. It has oolichan and other animals, and an eagle on top with mirrors in place of eyes. When the totem pole was taken up to Kemano Village, it was in September.[104] It was foggy, and somehow the sun burned through. The tide comes close to the pole and when the totem pole was raised up, the sun's reflection in the water hit the eagle's eyes, and like an eagle it would blink.

Jean says, "It is alive, Cecil. The pole is alive." Carver of the watchman and that is what this eagle is.

The breakwater, when I sit and walk along it, I feel the gratitude for Jean-Louis LeMay. His ability to change his attitude towards environment and the people who love the environment that make some seeds for change; that in my short lifetime I have witnessed destruction and I have witnessed a change. I will never see it completely change, but the beginning has started. How do we carry it on? How do we keep telling industry, not with anger, not with roadblock? The largest untouched rainforest that we saved with no roadblock. I keep telling my people, "Negotiate in good faith, with easy language, no cursing. Got to tell them who you are. Sometimes if you go in with anger, you make an avalanche with all that noise." The change in attitude of industry was beautiful. After that we found the survey markers.

A Daughter that Flew Away Long Ago

One winter night, I got a call from my sister Louisa who lives in Prince Rupert. She said she had a telephone conversation with a minister, John Cashore, and his wife Sharon, who they met when he was the United Church minister in Port Simpson. The minister asked her if she knew a person by the name of Cecil Paul. She said, "There's something I'd like to share with you." John and Sharon Cashore knew that Louisa was a Haisla. They were close friends in Port Simpson.

I said, "Go ahead and share."

Cecelia was near her 30th birthday when she went on that journey in search of who she is. She knew she was adopted. She found her mother was not 50 miles away from Cecelia all these years. And she met her mom who told her that "Your father is Haisla." She told John Cashore, her adopted father, who phoned my sister, Louisa.

I told Louisa, "Make contact; I dreamt about this." I told my wife, I told her my journey: "I have a daughter that flew away long ago."[105]

You're Walking in My Moccasins, the Father of My Child

Amazing part was John [Cashore] became a politician. He was an Environmental minister, later an Indian Affairs minister, and that's when we first met him, fighting for the Kitlope.[106] Gerald said that when he called the ministry up, they sent John up, Environmental minister. What it was like when I met this man that was the father of my child and holds the title, Environmental minister of BC, which includes the Kitlope?

What it was like to talk to him? What it was like when I first met the man that raised my child, that hugged her, that put Band-Aids on her feet when she had a scratch?

I remember the first acquaintance when my sister and I, Louisa, went down to Vancouver to meet Cecelia, and it seemed forever we were in separate rooms and then Cecelia was ready to see me. Without hesitation I felt the blood connection, I embraced. We talked for about four hours. My sister said, "I made arrangements that her parents are there, going to meet us." We went home to where Cecelia was waiting.

I asked my sister, "What gift are we going to give to a person who raised a child? Maybe a little flower, okay, that sounds good. You bring a flower and you give it to John, and I'll bring a little flower to give to her mom, that sounds good." We didn't know how to act; we didn't know what to expect.

John and Sharon weren't sitting together, they were sitting in two chairs, and I was the first one to speak and I told to the both of them, and I stressed it too, "I come here not to take your daughter away. I come here if you will have a compassion to share your child with me." The two of them came, we embraced and we cried, a little laughter here and there through the tears. I looked at these two women, at this man and wife, you've raised my child so beautifully. And that's how I addressed John, the father of my child, and I feel comfortable with it. I asked John, "How do you feel?"

And John said, "She's our child."

Sharon says, "Ours."

That was beautiful. I needed to hear that.

Cecil Paul in the Kitlope with daughter Cecelia Reekie, 2017.
BRIAN FALCONER

Sharon Cashore, Cecelia Reekie, Cecil Paul,
Marguerite Demers, John Cashore, 1991.
CASHORE FAMILY

And to Cecelia I say, "You are what I hungered for." I close my eyes and I said, "I think I see your father behind you. He's with you and your mom."

When I learned of her father – you know this residential school too was run by the United Church of Canada and that's where Minister Cashore was before he became the minister of the Environment – the question comes back of mistrust. Remember I talk about mistrust? That was quite a thing in my short life. The torture and abuse I got. It was the United Church of Canada who ran Port Alberni Indian Residential School. And who would I meet that raised my child? It was the United Church minister. From a person that was abused. And the hatred was planted in my heart of mistrust and hate.

United Church. And I stand in front of a person who raised an Indian child. My child. Cared for her.

You try and understand and condemn a whole United Church. Not only me, but hundreds and hundreds of people went to residential school. Coqualeetza Hospital was run by United Church. I brought that up at the Truth and Reconciliation conference in Vancouver. I told my story of learning how to forgive. White person didn't want me to marry his daughter, and the father wanted to kill the Indian child, and more hatred come. I lost five years. Then we finally met, and I learned that her father and mother were the United Church minister. I close my eyes, you know. One has to live through it to try to understand. I think that was the beginning of this wounded spirit on another healing journey.

When I first went up to the Kitlope with John, there was that trust. I said, "John do you think they will save the Kitlope?" I remember asking the father of my child, and I remember the smile on his face. That was quite a question to ask a minister: "Are you leaning towards saving the Kitlope?"

I think his answer was, "I think it's an appropriate thing to do, and to gain trust." There's that word again, to gain "trust."

I looked at this man, I says, "You're walking in my moccasins, the father of my child."

I told Gerald the whole story, just him and I and Louisa. "What I'm afraid of: Is it going to hurt our cause? Is it going to hurt Cecelia's dad? Everything's going to go against him in a question period. Or if we win the battle, will this degrade him? People will say, 'He done that because Cecelia's father's a Xenaksiala,' and I don't want John to get hurt. How can we save him? He done so much for me. We could ask for another minister to come up. Not the Environmental minister. We could ask his secretary or..."

"No," they said. "Let's face it ... let's talk to John. See what he says." Not a word was mentioned. Lots of emotions in my journey. I have pictures of him and me and Gerald sitting on the riverbanks of the Kitlope.

Final Decision Kitlope

Twenty minutes before the announcement – the government was going to announce that the Kitlope was going to be saved – (they gave us a little room in the part of the building where we were debating who was going to talk and who was going to open) and there was a knock on the door. A young man went to go answer it and he gave me a piece of paper and on it said, "Kowesas will not be safe." They took it out of the agreement. All this, 20 minutes before the announcement. The delegation with the Xenaksiala/Haisla got up to leave. They were so disheartened by what happened.[107]

I would not leave my chair. Everybody was at the door to walk away and tell the government to go to hell. But my little sister stayed. "Well, what is the matter with them?" I didn't answer her. Then the chiefs came, and they all got their seats back. This is a big surprise, but I knew something was going to happen today.

I said, "We should appreciate and enjoy what little time they have given us, and the people around the universe; we won a little battle. Let's accept what they offer us, and we'll rest for a year and then begin to fight again." It was a debate around the table, and then they said okay. They accepted, they took it.

Kenny Hall, hereditary chief of the Kowesas, he gave me the authority to walk on this land. He's the grandson of the fellow I told you about, Billy Hall, the man who saw the *bek-ʷus*, Sasquatch. This place here was part of the Kitlope that we fought for. There was only a five-year moratorium on this place. It was almost up, and they could have started logging again, but the moratorium kept adding five years. This one was done by labour and love.

More Good Journeys
in the Magic Canoe

1995–2018

Welcome Home Ceremony

A year goes by after the Kitlope was saved. One day Cecelia phoned and she said, "I'm coming up, Dad. I'm coming up with my husband, one grandchild – your grandchild, my father [John Cashore] and mother [Sharon Cashore]."

I said, "Okay."

I met Cecelia when they landed. Somebody came and said, "Your daughter is over there." I waited so long for that young girl that flew away from the nest, at that moment, separated by so many feet. I embrace my daughter. "Great Spirit, thank you. Thank you, Great Spirit."[108]

Cecelia receiving her name with Aunt Louisa Smith
and her father, Cecil Paul, Kitamaat, 1995.
CASHORE FAMILY

Cecelia never met her grandmother, my mum, but she knew she was going to come back. I have some pictures of when I introduced her to the Haisla people – her and John Cashore. I says to Cecelia, "If the hereditary chief gets up and touches you, means he is going to welcome you. He might not say a word."

The hereditary chief got up. I watched him with his arms around my little girl. Ah, I weep with joy. It was something. My auntie was the one who drummed and said, "Welcome home." And her daughters are two doors from here, Auntie's children. John Cashore came up to see the places where he raised the little girl and be welcomed by her people back home. All the miles he must have went through with my little girl.

Eighty-seven Steps: Forgiving the Church

I think that mostly people of my age have a little difficulty of accepting things have turned 'round for them. Can you forgive everything in your journey? It might be another person. From the back of my house here to the front door of the United Church, is 87 steps.[109] I still never stepped inside, and I never go. The United Church of Canada tormented me and hurt me bad, and the church of prayer is right here. I have still got something right here that I can't get rid of it. Some of my people are suing the United Church of Canada and the government. They ask me why I don't sue. But that is not my way. If I am going to get well, I need to forgive. Eighty-seven steps.

When we finally won the battle for the Kitlope, they were gonna start the Watchmen, Nanakila – caretakers of the Kitlope, Haisla.[110] And my boy was one of them, Cecil Junior. It had never dawned on me, what's going to happen. None of these Haisla or us had the experience caretaking something. It was taken away from us for how many centuries? Now put it in our lap again. Here you go. We had no experience. I talked to Gerald about it: "Let's get the chiefs together."

Brian [Falconer] came to ask me what is it going to be like for him in the Kitlope. He knew that we're in a journey that we have never travelled before. Of taking responsibility that's put in our land, of how we're going to conduct ourselves to share the beauty of the most untouched rainforest in the world. We could be thinking we are above our white brothers, white sisters, or we welcome with open arms and tell 'em, "We got the law here. All we want you to do is follow it. That's all we're gonna ask." I had to prepare my boys, when they get the uniform. It's amazing, once you have been underneath the feet of the government and then they give you a uniform, the power you feel inside has to explode. And an explosion is no good.

One day, this couple came up to Kemano, they were going to the United States, so they asked me to come along for a couple of months. We went to all the parks in the states starting in Seattle, all the way down, and I met all the young people who have uniforms working for the parks. I met all nationalities, having coffee with them. That is why I took the ride around all the parks, all the nationalities; your mind and heart are not separated by race or colour. My boy was one of the first to wear a uniform, and I told them what my brother said from Haida Gwaii: "Welcome each one with grace and tell them this is our law. No alcohol, pick up all the garbage. Simple little things."

Fishing Licences: The Government Lowering Us Down

Fresh prawns, halibut, it is so important to go out and relax on the ocean with a beautiful fresh fish. There are only four of the prawn fishermen left from the central coast: Bella Bella, one from Hartley Bay and two from Port Simpson. Anyway, there was seven Native people had licences, and my brother Dan Paul was one of them. Instead of calling it Indian licences, they call it "grandfather," but you cannot sell those licences.[111] They put that "grandfather" name on so that the Native people would be confused, the government lowering us down. The licence that they will sell to non-Native is quite high; Native licence is almost half. They had a real difficult journey. They had a few meetings. They called me down to Bella Bella to meet the people, and I didn't say a word. I didn't know nothing about prawn fishing. But what I heard was some painful things, the language they used, the government, concerning Native people for fishing. But that is the way it is.

A Gift that is Free: My Japanese Brother

In the old days, they wouldn't catch salmon for the winter until after they spawn. The male and females loses lot of its fat and they had bent boxes – see them in the museum – where they stack them up. When you think about it, that is conservation our people are doing. Letting them reproduce. The eggs lay and then they take the fish after they have spawned when the flesh loses all of its fat. Without the fat it means it won't turn rancid in the boxes in January and February. They say in February, *Quo'xemt'swa,* when people will take the scraps of meat from the bottom of the box. It is the last time they take what they preserve from the fall before. The next fish that comes up is the steelhead. First salmon that will go up the river. Now they can take it to eat. Then oolichans come. Gift from the Creator. Spring salmon now. The flesh is still firm, but it will taste different when it is in the river. So the spring come early. Then the humps [pinks], dogs [chum] and coho. Coho is the last one that will come up. Last fish. Coho running until November. They made it so that our people never starved, always food. Our house burnt down in Kemano, with all the old bent boxes and artifacts in them.

They wanted to put a fish farm in Kitamaat. Without knowing too much about it, I opposed it. There was only the two of us, me and Russell Ross, who I was with in Alberni, opposing this fish farm. One hereditary chief of the Kitasoo – very good friend outside the political arena – he was for it 100 per cent. He seen his people with money in pocket and could bring money to put in a fish plant close by here: "What the hell is our alternative, Wa'xaid, to put a few dollars in our people's pocket?"

I tell him, "Hemas, I am not too far away from you, and I appreciate it if you lower voice when you address me." That was my opening statement. How can I penetrate to tell him how bad the fish farm is for the natural gift of the salmon? How do they interact? Is there going to be differences? I don't know. But let us find out the differences before we say okay. I am for putting money in people's pockets, but before I agree I want to find out what damage fish farming does to the natural fish – a gift that is free.

When you have a debate, you try to explain to people what happens. *K'uun q*^{w}*otla*. Did you hear? Maybe I didn't hear; I'm sitting right beside you, but it didn't go through. I told him, "There are many alternatives to keeping a foreign fish – the Atlantic salmon – in our land. Nobody knows too much about what the Atlantic salmon is going to do if it escapes and goes into the rivers. You have enough salmon from our Creator. Every year, these rivers are full. Why bring in farmed fish from the Atlantic and plant it here? What is the alternative? Build your own cannery and do Alaska black cod but not a foreign fish."

The Kitasoo invited us down to take a look. They took us out to the pens and there was a Native kid feeding the fish. I ask the kid, "When did you start working here?"

"Three days ago," he said.

"Who worked here before?"

He said, "A couple of white boys."

They hired the Native kids because they invited the Haisla and had promised that it would be all Native people working there. I went to the chief and asked, "What did the government promise? That all the Kitasoo would work?" In the plant, not one Kitasoo was working there. When I got close to the pens, I smelt something like the fur of a dog when it gets close to the fire. When I saw what the kid was feeding the salmon, the stuff smelled the same.

We went through the plant and put those white clothes on. We see all this white fish. "Why is it white fish?" I ask.

"These are for Japan. Those fish over there are red, ordered by Americans. They like the red flesh." How do they change the colour for Americans buying red fish and Japanese buying white? Playing god?

We had a little gathering, they fed us, and I said, "You taste that same dog smell from the feed in the salmon's flesh." When I got back to Kitamaat, I went and told each hereditary chief, one-to-one.

Five years, we fight the fish farms. That is when I got really close to David Suzuki.[112] Phoned him every day. I think he got tired of me. I learned to trust him because he was my Japanese brother. No matter what colour, there is no difference. It's the feeling, once you came into the arena and see what you are facing. David sent a young Native guy from Alert Bay who had videos underwater from the farms; the bad things coming into the farms, the sea cucumbers all dead below the nets. He showed it to the people. What did the company promise? It was the turning point.[113]

One springtime, David calls up and says, "Hey, Brother, get your regalia. We are going to go on a big trip." We flew to Juneau. He took me to his stateroom and told me, "We are going to stop in every village along the coast and I want you to ask each chief to welcome us in his land." We had to go to Masset first, then Rupert, Hartley Bay, Klemtu, last stop Bella Coola.

I told him, "You are a crazy Japanese-Canadian, my brother."

Tara his wife said, "What did you call my husband?"

I said, "Your honourable Japanese gentleman."

When we got to Bella Coola, there was a big friction in the village. There is a beautiful river and the council want to clear-cut it, but dogs [chum] go up there. The village was divided. A lot of people were unemployed. The hereditary chief said, "No, leave it the way it is. Once we clear-cut that river, how long will it take to feed our people again? The logging is going to kill our river and there will be no more fish." The hereditary chief was Lawrence King. After he came out of Alberni Residential School, his grandfather gave him that name, Chief Pootlass.

I say a prayer. I talked to the chief councillor who was the hereditary chief's brother. Then they had two little girls, each carrying a spring salmon. They were Salmon Clan, and the only way you could be a Salmon Clan was to be a twin. My friend came with a knife, and they cut out the hearts of the salmon. They were facing the river and they slowly turned 'round and they sang a song and threw the hearts back into the river: "Come back to the river."

That night, they had a dance, and Lawrence told me this song came from the Kitlope and the dancer was a Haisla girl. The drums started dancing. It was the first time I heard the Kitlope song and danced with her to hear the heartbeat of the Kitlope. The rhythm was there, the Kitlope part of my heart.

We witness the Bella Coola people and that's when they decide to save the river.[114]

Return of the G'psgolox Pole

After we won the case for the river, I went up to Kitlope alone and I meditate. Did it really happen? I remember my little granny telling me of a totem pole that was stolen. We would gather in our little grandmother's house and very faintly I would remember her stories about the old totem pole and how it was taken against our people's will. That was when the journey of the pole begun.[115] They weren't only going to destroy the Kitlope; they have already wounded it by taking the grave marker of a big hereditary chief from the Kitlope. And we don't know where it is. From my little granny, she said, "Look for it." I was ten years old when she told me that. Before the boat came in and they took me away and I ended up in Alberni. That was my parting thing with my little granny, "Look for the totem." And, it took me I don't know how many years to find it, and it was in Sweden.

My little sister and I talk about what I knew about it to my people, but very few people gave me help. I got a Christmas card from a friend from New York. "I have a young friend, works in New York," she says. "Maybe she could find it." She says, "I'll look." She sends me a Christmas card: "I couldn't find it." I spilled my guts out to a stranger in a coffee shop, and then I turned around and she was a beautiful young girl, Spanish, Montserrat Gonzales. I told her I was up in the mountains looking for a totem pole, and I can't go up there anymore. It's over the mountain; it's over there. I close my eyes sometimes and the green grass, and it's over there.

And she says, "Maybe I could be a help with this new technology? I'm the curator of this museum here."

Oh, this Spanish girl caught me with Spanish eyes. Took her ten years. In that ten years, when I left her in that little coffee shop, I forgot about her. But she didn't forget. Took her ten years to figure out where the totem pole is. She says to me, "I went further up the mountain," and what she found in the records was something awful. Swedish consulate was stationed in Rupert and the Indian agent that looked after my people in Kitlope was stationed in Bella Coola. What she found was the correspondence of these two men, on how to steal a totem pole. Wow. It was awful.

I said, "Itemize it down. I'm going to call two friends."

I called Sister Louisa. She was the school coordinator in Prince Rupert and I said, "It's important that you come."

And she said, "I'll be there on a certain date."

Gerald was still the chief because he was re-elected. I went looking for Gerald, I said, "I want to show you guys something."

And the day came, the three of us walked in. I remember I told the Spanish girl to itemize it down to how she found it. She had a little piece of paper. I said, "One of you read it out loud so the three of us could hear." The very first line is: "Ten years ago, Cecil and I went on a journey." I realize now that it was the mountain of waves going across the Atlantic Ocean. It was some big waves. I seen only big hills, you know why I couldn't walk on water, I couldn't go halfway. I'm in my canoe, trying to paddle, trying to look for it; I couldn't make it.

The negotiations for that totem pole to come back were something hectic. When they weren't going any place, then Gerald said, "What do you think if we offer them a replica in exchange for that pole?"

"I'm not the owner of that pole," I say. "Chief G'psgolox is, my older brother. We cannot do nothing without his consent."

So in that little room they say, "Phone your brother and tell him. See if it'll be all right."

I finally got through. I says, "We're in a dilemma here. We're standing still. Gerald suggested if we make a replica in exchange for your pole."

There was a moment silence, maybe three, four seconds. And my brother came on, "Whatever it takes. You go for it." And that was all we needed. And the next time we meet with the Swedish government, our little delegation put that on the table.

In our culture, when a big chief dies he makes two carpenters build it. And when the pole falls, it go back to womb of Mother Earth. When that thing is almost decayed and back to the womb of Mother Earth, the new chief will take G'psgolox name, and he will build another totem pole. Now when they have taken this totem pole and cut it down, my culture believes – strongly believes – that they could never raise it up again. It's against our law, our *nuyem*, built into our mind. And we had a hard time with the Swedish government because they wanted us to make a museum. When I had our people together, I say, "Look at our land! No ships come in, this is the end of the road. And if you're gonna build a museum, it's got to have proper heat and things. We'd need a lot of people to pay a few dollars to come. No way can you keep a building to do what the Swedish government wants us to do." So I asked, "Come aboard my way of thinking and refuse those conditions." My government was still trying to raise money for a museum, but we couldn't find no funding.

Quite a debate about that, finally the Swedish museum say, "Okay, we'll let you take it back."

And when we came back, the little totem-pole committee said, "Dan and Cecil will go get the trees for the totem poles. We need two poles." I'm old; I couldn't climb around a mountain anymore. I had a friend, Bill Munro, who works for West Fraser who have the tree-farm licence for the Kitlope. We had to figure out the funding to pay for the totem poles. Who's going to carve it?

Still the Swedish government didn't understand what a totem pole means to our people. "Why do you want that old pole? Why don't you keep that replica that you are going to give us and put it back where the graveyard is?"

I said, "That's the difference between a museum and our Indian culture. You have stolen this from our graveyard. Its roots are there. The people that carved it could feel the sweat, the calluses on their hands building this totem pole. It don't belong in a foreign land. Let us take it home; we'll give you the new one. In our culture what this totem pole was meant to be, is back to where Chief G'psgolox is buried." And that's why we brought it back up to Kitlope – and it's there now.

Two G'psgolox poles, one old and one new, Museum
of Ethnography, Sweden, March 2006.

SPENCER B. BEEBE, ECOTRUST

They put a replica up in Sweden, and the Swedish people came when they raised the other replica in Misk'usa. I was in the hospital here – I couldn't make it. Great-granddaughter of the consulate from Sweden came up to Kitlope. She came to visit me in the hospital, and we had a long talk. I say, "I forgave your great-grandfather long ago. I forgave long ago." And there was something else. That original totem pole I gave her permission to go and see. Today the old pole has been set free. It is no longer in shackles. Bringing cultures together. We are all one creation.

The Spanish girl who found the pole in Sweden, Montserrat Gonzalez, was at the museum for seven years then she disappeared, and no one has heard from her since. We wanted to thank her. I ask people to try and find her like the totem pole, but nothing turn up.

Can I smoke? More than half-dead and I am still smoking.

Last Trip with Brian

I got a phone call. I knew in his voice he was suffering inside – Brian. "I'm halfway across Hecate Strait," he says. "I'm going to put the boat down in Vancouver Island and it is the last time I'm going to sail on it."

I said, "What are you telling me?" I ask. "Are you selling the boat?"

He said, "Yes. Will you come with me?"

No hesitation. "When do I have to be in Rupert?"

He gave me the time. "I'll be waiting for you."

I stayed with Louisa. When the time was right, they drove

Cecil Paul, in front of G'psgolox pole
replica at Misk'usa, April 2006.

KEVIN SMITH, MAPLE LEAF ADVENTURES

me down. Just him and I left Rupert, sailed all the way. Talked, he cooked for me, I cooked for him. It was miles and miles of quiet, but to me it was loud. The silence was loud. I look at my brother, all that love he had for that boat. He had repaired it from the old fishing boat; all the people he took around, taking all the environmentalists all over the coast, now his last trip and I had the honour for him to call me halfway across Hecate Strait, for the last trip. And for me too. Brother, it is a beautiful battle.[116]

Brian Falconer and Cecil Paul in the Kitlope, 2017.
BRIONY PENN

The Supertanker Has No Respect at All

One day, Gerald said, "You got *The Province*? Vancouver newspaper?"

"No," I say.

Gerald says, "Come over right away. It is a captain from India quoting that this channel will be the safest route to Canada. This captain never came into BC waters."

When I come I said, "Read it to me slow. What is this captain's name? Got his address? You know who could help us? Maybe Captain Brian, a person who came into our shores and can tell how the north wind can blow 100-130 miles an hour in a small funnel like that through the mountain, and if you got a big supertanker coming in with 2 million barrels of oil in it. If you got 12 big tugs trying to keep it out, there is no way you could beat Mother Nature. You got to get Brian; he knows about it. He knows the value of the wind. How can you navigate a supertanker into a narrow channel?[117] The supertanker has no respect at all."

LNG (Liquified Natural Gas): It Is Still Damage

Two pipelines gonna go down to my country. I go to the meeting as I was concerned about the pipeline. I heard the money talk first and then the environmentalists. The hereditary chief, Hemas, asked me, "*K'uun qʷotla?* Did you hear what they said? What is your vision of what you heard?"

When I first heard about it, I tried to talk to a friend who is a really good scientist. I was very uncertain about LNG, but in my heart I knew.[118] I phoned David Suzuki. I said, "David, explain to me little bit what is the difference between the oil and gas. On the left hand is oil. I am afraid of that. I am 100 per cent against oil pipeline. On the right hand is natural gas, and in my crazy mind it tells me it will evaporate into the air and the other will sink to the ground and the bottom of the ocean. How do I stand?"

David says, "There is less damage with natural gas but phone me back in 20 years." So, I think: less damage…less damage. They are buying us out if we allow these industries to come in, the garden is destroyed, all for that mighty dollar. And we are so blinded by the dollar. How do we tell our people to think about our garden? A lot of them opposed my way of thinking. And that was my journey.

My little sister Louisa and Murray Smith, they are fighting the LNG at Lelu Island with the other hereditary chiefs of Port Simpson.[119] Murray said at a meeting [with] the federal government, "Chairperson, what is this meeting about? It is supposed to be us telling the government our stories in our country and it is reversed. Government thinks, *They are only Indians; they don't know what the hell they are saying.*"

My little sister calmed things down: "I know you're working for the mighty dollar, but I want you to hear our voice. We don't want to take away your bread and butter, but look what you're going to take away – our whole world."

Sesek'as, Sitka Spruce: There Is a Story We Can Learn

Those big spruce, *sesek'as*, are washed down the river. The river got the trees by its roots, bounce them up and down. We say the Creator is making the riverbed soft for the salmon to spawn in the spawning ground. Cultivating where the salmon swim. The roots soften up the sand, so the male salmon will go like that. Preparing for his children to come and reproduce. This tree is one of the gifts of creation, to soften up the river, even when dead.

The pitch, our people use for a wound that will not heal. The pitch you mix with the bud of the cottonwood, which is oily. You mix it together, so it will not stick on the skin when you use it for medicine to heal. Our people have experienced it and carried the grief and the stories, told a chief from the Kitlope. He had a trapline way up in the bush and there was a big spruce up there, and he had seen an animal, a sea lion, and it had a wound on the neck and putting pitch on there to heal the wound. I have shot a black bear with pitch on it and birds. All the animals use it to heal their wounds. If you have a boil, it will heal it. Now the Xenaksiala/Haisla people will use it.

There was a guy who went to granny. He had fish poison and they wanted to take his hand off, amputate his hand, and he heard about my little granny and he went all the way from Rupert to Kemano/Kitlope, and my grandmother healed it. For two weeks they change it, and all the ugly things come out. One month later, he went to the doctor. The doctor said, "How did you heal it?"

And he said, "The person who healed it told me not to share."

When I first got sick, they removed the lower lobe of my left lung; I had cancer. Johnny and Bea Wilson came. They said,

"Drink this when you were thirsty." When my friends heard about it, they made a medicine, and now I am healed, by a different medicine for this cancer.

There is a tree down the path that is about love. It is a cedar and spruce joined at the roots and trunk, but they split halfway up to become spruce and cedar. There is a story we can learn.

Cottonwood: *Kalikula*. You've Had Enough

In July, you know the cottonwood trees? The inner bark is ready in July. We call it *luu'kwaxʷ*. You scrape it off. You know the coleslaw we eat in the restaurant? It taste exactly like that. Sweet. Dessert. You couldn't keep it long. The watery sap is *xwä yau*. It is in July too when the sap is running good. I haven't tasted that for a long time. The last time I tasted that, my sister and first cousin made it. She got married in Klemtu, said, "Brother, I got a present for you. Here eat it, with eggs of fish." You can only harvest the bark when the sap is running and after that the tree says, "*Kalikula*. You've had enough."

Stone Hunter: T'ismista

I close my eyes and go back to T'ismista,[120] our legend, our history of the man who turned to stone and the story behind him. It is the most important one of all the legends in the Kitlope that I use to tell the students that go up to Kitlope Lake. Like the college kids in Terrace who come up and go to the largest classroom in the universe, and I take them to this place. We are all children of the Great Spirit. No matter if you are 18 years old and have never heard the teaching of a Xenaksiala chief of how we came to be.

T'ismista is a hunter looking for mountain goats, that young guy who didn't listen. He was ambitious; he wanted to go and went against his Elder's teaching that he wasn't supposed to go up. He climbed up the mountain and got stuck on the ridge above Kitlope Lake. He whistled for his dogs. They went off. You can see one at Kemano and one at Mussel Inlet. The moral part of that story is that he did not listen. I tell my children and grandchildren that you will not turn to stone like that man, but you will go to the womb of Mother Earth before your time unless you listen to your teacher, your grandparents, your parents. Look at the newspapers of my people dying with overdose because they did not listen to their teachers.

T'ismista the stone hunter that didn't listen
to his elders above Kitlope Lake.
GREG SHEA, MAPLE LEAF ADVENTURES

T'ismista has a big hood that covers his eyes. In the month of June, on the longest days of the year, he reveals his face. You see his nose, his eyes and his lips. There are two mountains like that, and the sun will come down in the middle. It is the only time it is not in the shadow. Two times in my journey, I have seen his face. The story of T'ismista. Where we can see T'ismista, this is where sockeye spawn, all along here. They spawn close to the shore.

When we took the college kids up the Kitlope, we take the boats and go over with the paddles. I say, "Focus on that man. Focus on T'ismista." T'ismista's footprint is on the rocks going up at Qalhamut, and there is a little place further up, a rock on the trail where he sat down, and this rock fits every shape of bum. A big guy fits right. Young girl maybe 100 pounds fits just right. When you ask people, "How come they all fit the same?" I get a smile on my face. Then there is a hole in the ground that is never filled. Every time I go up when it rains, sand and stuff should cover it over, but it never has.

Kenny Hall went up in the helicopter to see where the Kitlope starts, and they took me up. We went from where the river starts rights down to the water. At that time there are some big amounts of snow. We were thinking about the ecotours starting at the head and going down to the Gardner. The helicopter came really close to T'ismista. Everyone had those earphones they talk to one another with, and in my language I told Kenny, "This bee is buzzing too close. Don't go too close." Everyone had their camera going and at once all them cameras stopped working, then all the cameras go on again, at the same time.

We got back to Kitamaat. Dr. Pritchard and Gerald came over carrying a big TV: "You got to see this, got to see this, Cecil."

You could hear my voice saying, "This bee is buzzing too close." Then the picture stops.

Daughters

One day, wintertime, Cecelia called: "You better come down, Dad. I have a flight for you on the plane. Maudie is really sick." So I got on the late plane, they paid my way, waited for me. Here my daughter, Maudie, she had a heart attack and her heart stopped. But the paramedics got it going again. It's the last resort anyway, so they done it really rough and they broke one of her ribs, but the heart worked again. She was all right. I met the two nurses who helped her.

When I went down there and stayed the doctor told us that it will be okay. And then she says, "Dad, if I live three or four days, I talked to Dave. I want to get married. Right here, right now."

And her older sister says, "Well, why not?" So she got the Justice of Peace, the doctors and the nurses. They didn't know if she was going to live, but she wanted to.

She said, "Dad, I look the Creator in the eye, I have no shame in mine. The way I feel about this man."

I says, "You gonna get better, woman!"

She had a little wedding cake. Her sister, Cecelia, they look alike. How can one put them into words of how a dad feels for a young daughter they took away from me for years. Two other girls that I've lost, almost lost another in my lifetime, but she came and got me.[121]

TRC: The Weight Lifted from My Favourite Canoe

There was an election for school board and Cecelia won. She's the first Aboriginal, first Native, to go on the school board in Langley, BC.[122] And it was my daughter. Now her work is educating people about the TRC. I watched the TRC Panel all day on the TV. It will never heal this generation, maybe my great-grandchildren. I talked 30 to 40 minutes, saw old Buffy Sainte-Marie. I met a young man from Port Simpson who said that I gave him the courage to go back. Come and talk about the pain. Talked most, when I am invited to go. I always talk about residential schools. I have reached someone from the darkness.

I'd never met him, Wab Kinew, before, but he was giving a talk at the school that Cecelia works at; Cecelia asked him to go. "Okay. I'd love to go." I don't know how long we drove, but we made it to this little reserve and there was an Elder sitting by the door and children and a lot of visitors. He opened the thing with his own language then translated, introducing the young man to the crowd. He talked in his mother tongue. Then he spoke English after that. What really impressed me was the Elder sitting there, quiet, and he introduced Wab Kinew in his mother tongue. I got the weight lifted from my favourite canoe.

Son: Take Me Home

My boy has many years of sobriety. Him and Gerald's boy really hit it off together. They trust one another. Good to have a partner to trust. Everyone loses trust, lied to too many people. I took him out since he was six. Made a bed for him. He helped me fish. I ask him, "Do you remember the bend in the river? Remember the tree that you see on the right-hand side?" The third year, he was nine, and I didn't tell him why but said, "Make me a bed. I'm going to lie down, and take me home." He took me from Kitlope Lake back to Kitamaat.

Top, left to right: Gerald Amos, Kenny Hall, Cecil Paul Jr.;
Bottom, left to right: Cecil Paul, Louise Barbetti,
Dan Paul, Louisa Smith, 1994.
SPENCER B. BEEBE, ECOTRUST

I tried to teach him how Johnnie Wilson and I were. How to be here at this point at a certain time, not ten minutes late, not half an hour late, not 20 minutes early, and then you give up or he is late and then you leave, and they come up and check. You have to program your mind when you tell anybody when you're leaving.

Grandson: Take His People from A to B with No Shame

The government almost succeeded in brainwashing us. They failed Russell Ross and I because we defied the order and went underground. Now, when you think about this generation, did they succeed? I'll use my household, my grandchild, as an example. I use mostly English when he comes and talks to me. Once in a while I use my language: "Go get this for me; go get that," in my language. He hears somehow, but I'm not teaching him enough of my mother tongue. I'm using half and half. Penetrating another culture, another language. "Grandpa, come back to Grandpa's language." What's in his mind? I don't know.

My grannie had a sister called Alice, and Alice married a big chief, Hail from Kitkatla, and my granny married Chief Johnny Paul. The two sisters... and Granny gets lonesome for her sister and asks her husband, "I'll call her up to come oolichan fish with us?"

And the chief agrees: "Call your sister."

When she came, she brought along a little boy, his name is Russell Gamble. And my grandfather was so happy that they were coming that he made a totem pole for that nephew, his

Cecil's sisters, Louisa Smith and Vietta Wilson, with
Cecil Paul Jr. and Thomas Paul, Cecil Paul's grandson,
in their herring punt, Kemano, March 2008.

CECIL PAUL

name was Dla la xii la yewx. Only him can control the direction his boat wants to go. He is the chief that will take his
people from A to B with no shame, with no hunger and no battle. It will probably be a chief that will do good to his people.

I have given Dla la xii la yewx name to my grandson. His
name is Thomas Paul. It was my wife who negotiated the
name to transfer it, to come back to the Kitlope, Dla la xii la
yewx.[123] When people address my boy in the feast, they call
him Hemas Dla la xii la yewx, Chief Dla la xii. He don't know
it yet, but somebody will tell him. I addressed all the chiefs in

the community: "You might see my grandson, Dla la xii, laying in the gutter, and if he don't listen, one of you have compassion; take him up. See if you could make him?" That is my wish to my people.

The Way He Speak My Language

I was going down to the marina to check the boat a few years ago, and there is one white guy. I hear this: "*'iks nakʷa*."
He is the only one there. I say, "I beg your pardon?"

And he says, "*'iks nakʷa*."

I say, "Who are you?" I shook his hand.

He says, "I am learning about the Haisla language." He said good morning to me in Haisla. His name was Emmon Bach.[124] That surprised me, and we became really good friends, with Louisa, my sister. Everything was beautiful the way he speak my language, that is why I didn't see him. I didn't see a Haisla Native, I saw a big white guy: "*'iks nakʷa*." It is amazing. Speaks so clear Haisla words. You have to dig deep down here to pronounce it.

She Is Your Queen

I'm watching the queen's 90th birthday. "I don't want to watch," I say.

Brian said, "Me too."

I says, "But try to go visit her. They won't allow us in their palace. Four chiefs try and go to England.[125] I wanted to ask the queen to apologize to the Canadian Natives. They done it for Australia, apologize, and New Zealand. Two. They won't even call my chief, have a cup of tea. Well, I don't want to see her. She is your queen."

That little girl, Jess Housty in Bella Bella, is something, meeting the queen's grandson. It takes the one you trust to write a letter to the queen, to her husband. Now we're fighting for the same thing, what the chiefs are meeting of the pipeline, and they have been through this before. Why they are going to put the pipeline through? And she questions: Is this wise? How many years have they celebrated the birthday of Canada and yet so many people know very so little of Wa'xaid and his people? Very few.

Lä g̈ølä's: Put Our Canoe Ashore and Rest

I told Gerald a few years ago, "Gerald I can't pull anymore. I am tired and sick. *Lä g̈ølä's*. Put our canoe ashore and rest. Build a fire; we'll have a meeting. Discuss. I will go back in the canoe, everybody again, and that was good. Take a look at us now. We must not forget: our gift of love is to protect. The protectors. It is a good journey."

I think that Magic Canoe, it was the beginning of a momentum of how we could paddle all in harmony. Okay, one more trip. Let's sit down and talk about how to put words in this Magic Canoe – the tree. Emphasize the love of all the people that came aboard of the canoe. One thing alone: it was the love of the environment. There should be no hard words to the ones who are fighting. Gotta talk in a soft voice and make them come aboard.

It's my son's turn, my daughter's turn. Cecelia fights for

the same thing, whether adopted, it's what she's doing now, so she's helping other people. This journey really helps a lot of people, the Kitlope, the pole itself, brought people from around the universe. All these things could have never happened alone, without beautiful friends who came aboard the Magic Canoe.[126]

P'ä nii Qwiid: The Sun Is Kissing the Mountains Good Night

When it was almost her time, my mother called Sister Louisa to her bed and said, "*Hadii Cecil giilxowd wax mass.* When Cecil goes to sleep, he is the one who is going to turn out all the lights [of Kitlope]." That was how many years before? I sit here and ponder.

So each day now, when I wake up and I see daylight, I say, "Great Spirit, let me walk softly today and not to hurt another human fellow traveller along my path." Tell your children and your grandchildren about this place and enjoy what you see. It is a garden, and we must protect it. I remember my granny and my mum having a chair like this, sitting in the Kitlope, enjoying this time as evening come. I hear my granny singing about the Kitlope. *P'ä nii qwiid.* The sun is kissing the mountains good night. Come, the Creator tells us, we are not alone. This is the Kitlope talking. I want to thank all of you who have left a footprint. I'm glad. Perhaps one day you will come here. Whatever the cause may be, whatever the journey is for us, we'll leave this place and hope that you'll carry the peace of Kitlope in your heart and pass it on to people. Your children,

"All of you who have left a footprint in the sand, I am glad." Grizzly prints, Kitlope River, May 2015.

GREG SHEA, MAPLE LEAF ADVENTURES

grandchildren. It is not impossible – always there is hope. Thank you for coming to my home.

"The sun is kissing the mountains good night," Kitlope, 2017.
MAPLE LEAF ADVENTURES

Short Chronology of Historic Events Described by Wa'xaid

c. 9,000 years ago   Waa-mis founds the Haisla/Xenaksiala settlements in the Gardner/Douglas area.

1763   Royal Proclamation.

1793   Europeans arrive: Captain George Vancouver and Alexander Mackenzie.

1831   Hudson's Bay Company establishes Fort Simpson.

1862   Smallpox brought to Fort Simpson, followed by gunboats.

1874   Founding of first residential school at Fort Simpson.

1890   Creation of the Indian Reserves around Kitamaat and Kitlope.

1892   Arrival of missionary school in Kitlope.

1917   Start of influenza epidemic.

1920   Indian Act makes it illegal to withhold an Indian child aged seven to 15 from attending school.

1929   G'psgolox pole taken from the Kitlope.

1931   Native Brotherhood founded. Guy Williams, Cecil's uncle, is an early leader in the Brotherhood.

1934   Canadian census conducted. 30 Kitlope people left.

1946   Miller Bay Hospital is finally opened for Indigenous people suffering from tuberculosis.

1947   Guy Williams, with the Native Brotherhood, goes to Ottawa to plead for revisions to the Indian Act.

1948   Amalgamation of Kitamaat (Haisla) with the Kitlope/Kemano villages (Xenaksiala).

1949 An Act to Promote the Industrial Development of the Province is passed, greenlighting Alcan and Kemano River diversion.

1958 Prince Rupert riot of over a thousand Indigenous people against discrimination.

1964 Gordon Robinson, Haisla leader, draws attention to impacts of pollution on the Kitimat River.

1965 Awarding of Tree Farm Licence 41 (Kitlope, Kemano, Kildala and parts of Kitimat watersheds) to Eurocan Pulp and Paper Company.

1978 Haisla file a comprehensive land claim. Premier Bill Vander Zalm comes up with the "solution" to ship "urban Indians" back to their reserves.

1980 West Fraser buys a 40 per cent interest in Eurocan and starts plans to log the Kitlope.

1987 Meech Lake Accord enshrines protection of "existing" Aboriginal rights.

1989 Boston Men and others start joining the Haisla in the Magic Canoe.

1990 Haisla serve injunction to Government of Canada against any more incursions.

1994 The Province of British Columbia and the Haisla Nation announce that the Kitlope will be fully protected and jointly managed.

1995 Kemano Completion Project is halted.

1995 Arthur Plint pleads guilty to 18 counts of sexual assault at Alberni Indian Residential School.

2000 Replacement for G'psgolox pole travels to Sweden.

2001 Chief Justice Brenner hands down a judgement on the Alberni case against the Government of Canada and United Church of Canada.

2006 G'psgolox pole returns to Kitamaat Village.

2010 Eurocan closes its doors permanently.

2010 Enbridge Northern Gateway Pipelines Ltd. submits application to National Energy Board for a port at Kitimat.

2011 LNG Canada buys old Eurocan plant for production of liquified natural gas and port.

2013 World Indigenous Network in Darwin, Australia, features Cecil Paul.

Cecil Paul and Maple Leaf guests at his Kitlope River cabin, Briony Penn recording, spring 2006.
MAPLE LEAF ADVENTURES

The Paul family, left to right: Maudie, Rhoda, Sophia (Rhoda's daughter), Cecil Jr., Mamie (Mae), Cecil Sr., Joyce, c. 1987.

Short Chronology
of Wa'xaid's Life

1931 Born on the Kitlope River.

1936 Taken to Elizabeth Long Memorial School then hidden by grandfather.

1941 Taken to Alberni Indian Residential School.

1945 Leaves Alberni Indian Residential School and goes to Butedale; starts drinking; first time in jail for sitting in white section of theatre in Prince Rupert.

1946 Working in Cumshewa, Haida Gwaii.

1947 Brother Leonard, father Tom Paul and two aunts die of TB.

1949 Brother Vincent Paul runs away from Alberni Residential School.

1951 Cecil blows off two fingers with his shotgun, flown to Prince Rupert from Kemano.

1952 On survey team of Kitimat River for transport corridor, caught in big flood.

1953 Starts fishing along coast with various types of fish boats and works in cannery.

1958 Working on railway track around Terrace.

1962 Brother Vincent Paul found dead.

1963 Daughter Cecelia is born to Marguerite Demers in Prince Rupert and taken to a foster home; she ends up with United Church Minister John and Sharon Cashore.

1963 Labours at Tulsequah, next five years in and out of prisons and labour jobs.

1966 Death of his granny, Annie Paul.

1967 Meets Patricia (Mae) Williams; three daughters and a son born in the next four years; works as longshoreman at Kitimat.

1970 Starts working for Eurocan on docks; marries Mae.

1971 Stops drinking, returns to the Kitlope and recovers his health; re-establishes oolichan camps with family.

1978 Finds voice in village speaking up about Eurocan's pollution in the Kitimat River and becomes a band councillor before health issues force him to step down.

1980s Starts fight against Kemano Completion Project and impact on oolichan.

1988 Works to stop erosion of the burial ground at Kemano.

1989 Cecelia contacts Parent Finders and finds her birth parents; Cecil meets John and Sharon Cashore.

1990 Finds survey markers in the Kitlope, start of four-year campaign in the Magic Canoe.

1994 Awarded the Hero of the Planet award from Rainforest Action Network.

1997 Travels to Sweden to continue to negotiate the return of the G'psgolox pole.

1999 Death of wife Mae.

2002 Death of daughter Rhoda.

2006 G'psgolox pole returns to Kitamaat.

2011 G'psgolox pole returns to the forest.

2013 Features at the World Indigenous Network in Darwin, Australia.

2015 Truth and Reconciliation Commission Report comes out.

2016 Death of daughter Joyce.

2017 Death of daughter Maudie.

Cecil Paul's Family
through the Matriarchs

WITH ASSISTANCE FROM CECIL PAUL SR.,
LOUISA SMITH, JAY POWELL
AND CHARLES MENZIES.

ALL MISTAKES ARE THE AUTHOR'S.

Legend: = union/marriage; > child; – grandchild; {} grandchildren

Annie Morrison, Wii'deałh, Salmon Clan (1870 – 1966)
(When Wa'xaid mentions his granny, it is Annie, Wii'deałh. Her play name was Muk'waxdi – "constantly following closely behind.")

= #1 Samuel Wilson (? – 1917?) (died of influenza)

> Lizzie (? – 1947?) (died of internal complications)

> Agnes (1898 – 1947) (died of tuberculosis)

> Charlie, Wä wii no yew wa (1900 – 80)
(When Wa'xaid mentions Uncle Charlie, it is this Charlie, aka Dad.)

> Thomas (Tom), Gwä nax nood (1906 – 47)
(Tom is Wa'xaid's father. Tom was adopted by his aunt, Esther Wilson, Samuel Wilson's sister. Her family tree is below. She married Charles Paul of Kitkatla. Tom died of tuberculosis.)

= #2 Johnnie (also Johnny) Paul, Chief Humzeed of Raven Clan (1887 – 1947)

(Annie lost her second husband, and three of her children by her first marriage, in one year during the epidemics of 1947.)

> Minnie (1909 – 98) = Guy Ronald Williams (Kitamaat)

> Louisa (1913 – ?) = Edmond Smith (Kitamaat) {children including Crosby, who took Wa'xaid's father, Thomas Paul's, name, Gwä nax nood.}

Clara Thompson, Hay xʷäks, Eagle Clan (1901 – 80)
(Agwii was her play name.)

= Thomas (Tom) Paul, Gwä nax nood (1906 – 47) (see notes on Thomas Paul below)

> Emily, Gwalask (1922 – 2005) = Joe Daniels (Kitwanga)

> Joe (1923 – 48) = Edith Wilson (drowned in Kemano)

> Jimmy (1925 – ?) = Ruth

> Leonard (1927 – 47) (died in Miller Bay Hospital from TB)

> Cecil Donald, Wa'xaid, adopted into Killer Whale Clan (November 28, 1931)

= #1 Marguerite Demers (1947) (no marriage, Butedale)

- Cecelia, Nuyem dzeets 'iksduqʷia (June 4, 1963) (adopted by John and Sharon Cashore) = Dave Reekie {Dave and Chris}

= #2 (Mamie) Patricia Williams (1947 – 99)

- Rhoda Sheila (May 5, 1967 – July 24, 2002) = Earlin Bolton {Sophia}

- Maudie Darlene, Gwiiyms Moodzill (June 12, 1968 – August 2, 2017) = James De Kleine (no marriage) {Christopher}

        = Dave Koenders

- Joyce Cecilia (July 4, 1969 – September 29, 2016) = Pete Smith {Chelsea, Thomas}

- Cecil Charles, Jr. (December 4, 1970) = Karen Smith

> Douglas (1933 – 2006) = Nora Hunt

> Daniel Thomas, G'psgolox (1934 – 2014) = Edith Cross

> Vincent Harry (1936 – 62) (drowned at Port Edward)

> Florence (1938 – 2000) = Robert Fowler (Kitwanga)

> Louisa, Amalaxa (1939) = Murray Smith (Port Simpson)

> Vietta Linda (1944) = Bernard Wilson

Esther Wilson (? – 1917) (sister of Samuel Wilson)

= Charles Paul, Gwä nax nood (c. 1878 – 1918)

(Both Esther and Charles died during the influenza epidemic of 1917 – 18.)

  Thomas (Tom) Paul (1906 – 47)

  (Tom was adopted by his aunt and uncle. He was the natural son of Annie, Wii'deałh, and Samuel Wilson, brother of Esther Wilson. The reason Charles Paul adopted Tom was to continue the name Gwä nax nood. Tom was paid the Wä xox^w river (Kemano) by Johnnie Livingston in return for a deed.)

Sara (??) Kitlope (possible lineage based on Johnny Paul's death certificate)

= Abraham (Abel) Paul, Wa'xaid, Killer Whale Clan (? – 1925)

(Abel is Charles Paul's brother and Wa'xaid's uncle by adoption. The name Wa'xaid that was passed on to Cecil Paul came from Abel. He and Charles Paul are whom Wa'xaid refers to as "the mysterious brothers from Kitkatla." It is thought that Chief Paul [Sheaks] could be their father, also believed to be a name brought from Kitkatla.)

  Johnnie (also Johnny) Paul, Chief Humzeed of Raven Clan (1889 – 1947)

Endnotes

BRIONY PENN

The recording and transcribing of Wa'xaid's stories and re-searching the endnotes that follow are the culmination of a 25-year friendship. In 1992 I was one of the many to climb into the Magic Canoe to help the Haisla/Xenaksiala (hereafter Haisla) fight for the Kitlope. The first time I met Wa'xaid was to attend his lecture on the Kitlope. I sat in the dark in a packed auditorium in Victoria mesmerized by Wa'xaid's vision of protecting his home – the largest unlogged, temperate rainforest watershed on the planet. Those who witnessed the Haisla at that evening lecture were drawn by the power of their stories and kinship to the land. Enviro-types like me stepped easily into the canoe to find guidance from those steering it. About five years after that lecture, I had the privilege to work with him when I was a naturalist aboard the schooner *Maple Leaf*, through our mutual friend, Brian Falconer. Wa'xaid mentored me through the Kitlope and the coastal nations through which we travelled together. We sailed along the trajectory of his life: a labourer in a mine near Juneau, a fisherman in Prince Rupert, a longshoreman in Haida Gwaii, a cannery worker in Butedale, a student at Alberni Indian Residential School, a drunk in Vancouver's downtown east side, an inspiring mentor and leader in the Kitlope. I got to meet some of the other leaders on the coast, who I later learned were his fellow survivors of Alberni. He is friends with everyone, from the waitresses in the fishermen's cafes to the David Suzukis and the Rockefellers of the world. I watched how people opened their hearts and minds after exposure to Wa'xaid's teachings.

Over the years, we started to hear about "the arrows" of his life: the residential schools, the germ warfare, the land grabs, the herding into reserves, the Indian hospitals, the imprisonments – physical and mental, the withholding of justice or medicines, the poisoning of rivers. These accounts came from someone who not only had experienced these arrows first hand but, through the teachings of his culture, had overcome his anger with an indomitable spirit of friendship for anyone who turned up to help. In spending time with Wa'xaid, I also got an inkling of the snubs and petty discourtesies of my culture, the daily grind of prejudice. I had the typical settler response of getting angry for him when he wasn't. Given that my ancestors were the judges and politicians that crafted the laws that harmed him, his friendship was a precious gift. It went further than that; Wa'xaid taught me to "penetrate" the mind of my ancestors and see their humanity. His belief that we are all connected – from the dogfish in the murky estuaries to their equivalent in the CEOs of oil companies – isn't abstract. It is a worldview that is transformative when you witness the power of it.

Wa'xaid felt that these written records would provide the dates and facts to form a framework for Western readers, should they need one. The extended family tree that grows from the matriarch Annie Paul, Wa'xaid's grandmother, can be found after Wa'xaid's story. Family trees also tell stories. The colonial practice of only making it mandatory for white people to register births and deaths means that visits to graveyards sometimes provide the only resource for Indigenous family trees, where, if you are lucky, there are dates. A short chronology that marks events recorded in his stories is also included here at the back. When Wa'xaid says "you" in his stories, he is speaking to you, to me, to all of us – we are paddling in this Magic Canoe together. Our survival depends on it. I hope these stories encourage you to step into the Magic Canoe and join the many others for what I consider to be the greatest privilege of my life – following the Good River, Wa'xaid.

Introduction

1 Louisa Smith, Wa'xaid's sister, provided the spellings of her language using the International Phonetic Alphabet. She is one of the four last fluent speakers of Xenaksiala. Wa'xaid shared Xenaksiala words when there was no English equivalent, such as *Lä göläs'* ("put your canoe ashore and rest").

2 Xenaksiala lands (also written as Henaksiala) include the entire watershed of Gardner Canal, south and east of Kitimat, British Columbia. Part of that territory, the Kitlope watershed, at one million hectares, is the largest unlogged, temperate rainforest on the planet.

3 When Wa'xaid says, "they call it Kitlope," his "they" refers to European mapmakers, like Captain Vancouver, or their closest Tsimshian trading partners. Kitlope is a Tsimshian word for "people of the stone" because of the huge granite cliffs. The Tsimshian live north and west of the Haisla and Xenaksiala, largely along the Skeena River and out into the islands. The Tsimshian language, known by its speakers as Sm'algyzx, is a completely different language from that of the Xenaksiala. Wa'xaid and the Paul family have close ties to Tsimshian families.

4 Haisla territory covers most of Douglas Channel.

5 Gardner Canal is BC's longest inlet at 320 kilometres (200 miles).

Vancouver named it after his boss, Admiral Alan Gardner, who never saw it.

6 Of the *wa'wais* (watersheds, areas of stewardship, determined under traditional laws or *nuyem*) that pour into Gardner, the first is Crab River, which demarcates the beginning of the territory of the Xenaksiala people and the end of the Haisla *wa'wais*. Halfway along Gardner is the Kemano River, which is the *wa'wais* held by Wa'xaid and where the Kemano and Kitlope people officially "lived" until 1948, when the two villages amalgamated with Kitamaat to survive. In the colonial maps of British Columbia there was no indication of the 54 *wa'wais* boundaries of the Haisla and Xenaksiala.

7 River's Inlet is the English name for Wuikinuxv (Oweekeno, who speak Oowekyala). The linguistic group is described by linguists as Northern Wakashan, with four related languages: Haisla/Xenaksiala, Owekyala, Heiltsuk, and Kwakw'ala.

8 The late Gordon Robinson was a renowned Haisla Elder who wrote down some of the *nuyem* (code/laws of stewardship) and stories of the Haisla, published in 1956 as *Tales of the Kitamaat*. *Nuyem jees* is "the place where you get your ethics relating to the world." At least that is how Wa'xaid's friend and anthropologist John Pritchard describes it to people with a Judeo-Christian background: "Think of the *nuyem* as the Ten Commandments; Kitlope as Mount Sinai."

9 The Kitlope River flows into a lake, oval and luminescent with its milky-blue glacial water. Ice-caped mountains tower above this lake, and for that reason the Xenasiala call it *Ka-ous*. The closest Wa'xaid can come to translating that word into English is "cathedral," as it gives people a sense of the beauty, peace and awe you feel when you enter the lake from the river.

10 A coastal temperate rainforest is a forested area lying between 32 and 63 degrees latitude with over 2000 millimetres (80 inches) of precipitation (rain, fog or snow) per year. In 1991 the Kitlope represented 2 per cent of what was left on the planet of this threatened ecosystem.

One: So Many Arrows Came Our Way

11 Wa'xaid is referring to the time when he stopped drinking, July 18, 1971, which is when he started on his healing journey to regain his health.

12 Annie Paul, Wii'dealh, was born in the Kitlope in 1870 into the Salmon Clan. She died at the age of 96. Longevity was common in Xenaksiala people before colonization. The word *Xenaksiala* means "people who die off slowly," referring to their ripe old ages, not lingering diseases. Diseases, like smallpox, came later, but they weren't lingering. They hit the shores of Gardner Canal like tsunamis.

13 The first outbreak of smallpox on the north coast was May 25, 1862. By the following year, according to both Indigenous and non-Indigenous accounts, between 75 and 100 per cent, depending on the village, of all Indigenous people were dead. The influenza epidemic of 1917–18 took Annie Paul's first husband, Samuel Wilson, and her sister-in-law and brother-in-law, Esther and Charles Paul (of the Tsimshian Paul family) who had adopted Tom Paul, Wa'xaid's father. The tuberculosis epidemic in 1947 took her second husband, John Paul (of the Kitlope Paul family) and three of her six children: Lizzie, Agnes and Tom. Only Annie's two youngest daughters, Minnie and Louisa, survived the epidemics. Minnie went on to marry Guy Williams, who became the second Indigenous senator of Canada and a leader in the Native Brotherhood movement.

14 Kitamaat Band signees were Gordon Robinson (chair), Fred Woods, Ernest Grant, Heber Amos, Don Grant and Joseph Bolton. Kemano signees were Chief Simon Hall, Joseph Paul (older brother of Wa'xaid) and Gordon Robertson.

15 In 1949, Bill 66, An Act to Promote the Industrial Development of the Province, was passed, which greenlighted the building of the Kenney Dam, flooding the lands above the Kemano River, diverting waters into a tunnel blasted through the mountain into Wa'xaid's *wa'wais*. Western superpowers wanted a secure supply of aluminum for weaponry and planes, which required cheap electricity. Wa'xaid's *wa'wais* was the place they picked. The greenlighting of Alcan's $500-million (1951 cost) project rode conveniently (for the colonial powers) on the decision to consolidate the villages of Kitlope, Kemano and Kitamaat.

16 The document Wa'xaid is referring to was written by Inspector of Indian Agencies J. Coleman in Bella Coola, October 1941. Kitlope families had been taking up residence on the Kitamaat Reserve, and he wrote the words that so outraged Wa'xaid, "the only opposition apparently coming from the Chief of the Kitlope Band, who did not wish to relinquish his somewhat imaginary authority."

17 The documents were collected by Charlie Shaw, Wa'xaid's cousin by marriage. They include the 1934 Census of Indians.

18 The 1934 Census of Indians notes that the Kitlope (Xenaksiala) numbered 30, with a breakdown according to age and gender. There were only 2 Kitlope males under 7 years in 1934. Wa'xaid, born in 1931, was one and his brother the other.

19 Wa'xaid uses "little" to show a special endearment to a person he is close to, like his little granny and his little uncle.

20 According to Wa'xaid and his Elders, at least 700 people (some accounts refer to up to 3,000) used to live in the Kitlope before smallpox. In 1890 Peter O'Reilly, Indian reserve commissioner, local Indian agent, recorded, "the population of this tribe is 103." By 1934 it was 30.

21 All oral accounts and some Western historians regard the smallpox epidemic of 1862–63 as a premeditated case of germ warfare and genocide. Accounts of the "ugly blanket," in which germs were distributed, were passed down to Wa'xaid from his grandparents and other Elders, as were oral accounts of their own quarantines being broken down by military raids, opening up potential for infection. Also the use of false vaccinations with "the knife." These vaccinations, instead of applying cowpox to a wound with a knife, were actually inoculations of live smallpox, and, according to Shawn Swankey in his book *The Great Darkening*, could become "infectious … and pass the disease to others, starting epidemics" (p. 51).

22 The letter that Wa'xaid refers to is from Peter O'Reilly, Indian reserve commissioner, in the spring of 1890 on the newly created reserves of Kit-a-mat. Reserve No. 3, "*Waw elth* is situated about one mile south of reserve No. 2, and contains thirty-five acres. This is a site of an abandoned village; a number of small gardens surrounding the ruins of the old houses. A few inferior salmon are taken at the mouth of a small stream that flows through this reserve, and huckleberry and crab apples abound in the vicinity." He signs off: "I have the honour to be Sir, your obedient Servant P. O'Reilly."

23 The Xenaksiala and Haisla, who have occupied and owned this land for thousands of years, have always had their own forms of land stewardship of their huge territory, including logical units of watersheds or *wa'wais*. Boundaries follow the tops of mountains around the different drainage basins of the rivers. Every watershed has a name that corresponds to its

owner. The owners have both control and responsibility handed down through their mothers' lineage. Each owner is bound by the *nuyem*, a code of stewardship that has detailed prescriptions for how the land, waters and wildlife are to be harvested, shared and respected.

24 Oolichan are a small forage fish that, like salmon, bring the energy of a life at sea to the rivers during the great boiling hiatus of a spawn. In their reproductive state, they have packed on so much oil that when the Haisla boil them, the surface of the cooking water develops a slick. The oil was so valuable to First Nations that the trails between oolichan rivers and interior villages became major arteries. Corridors for moving oil are nothing new on the coast, and it was these grease trails that led the first Scotsman, Alexander Mackenzie, to the coast in July 1793, a week after Captain Vancouver cruised through. For Mackenzie, this journey was a stroll along a major trade route, hardly bushwhacking. Ironically, the route of the modern oil and gas pipelines – proposed twice in the last 30 years to link the oilfields with what oilmen call "tidewater" – lies along one of the traditional grease trails. Oil has always been a player in the history of this region.

25 Clio Bay (the Haisla name is Gwaxsdlis) is where HMS *Clio*, during a patrol, captured three American schooners selling whisky. The captains came under the unforgiving judgement of the missionary and lay magistrate William Duncan, the Methodist minister who had no patience for the alcohol trade. Duncan's heavy sentence on the men was appealed, and Judge Matthew Baillie Begbie reduced the severity of the fine. His decision displays the deeply ambivalent perspective of government regarding alcohol sales to Indigenous peoples, as it generated a lot of revenue. Two other accounts of why HMS *Clio* was up north include early *Vancouver Province* reporter Bruce McKelvie's version: to break up the "secret societies, ritualistic cults and savage practices." Another version from missionary Elizabeth Varley, in her book *Kitimat My Valley*, sides with the Haisla: "They [the Haisla] wanted none of the treatment the white man had handed out to other Indians. So HMS *Clio* was sent in as a threat, with the unspoken message: 'You trade or else!'"

26 See Wa'xaid's story "Return of the G'psgolox Pole." (It is also spelled Gps'golox.)

27 At the time Wa'xaid didn't know that more could have been done by the federal government to deliver streptomycin earlier to the Indigenous population. Like smallpox, tuberculosis was not just a natural disaster

that happed to affect Indigenous peoples in the manner it did. There were military, cultural and economic factors behind the policy that ensured a slow and ineffective rollout of TB treatments for Indigenous peoples. As Maureen Lux writes in her book *Medicine that Walks: Disease, Medicine, and Canadian Plains Native People, 1880–1940*, in 1937 the director of Indian Affairs, Harold McGill, "instructed agents to drastically reduce medical care. They were to remove from hospitals all Native people with chronic conditions. There would be no more funds for tuberculosis surveys or for treatment in sanatoria or hospitals of chronic tuberculosis."

It wasn't until after the war, on September 16, 1946, that the local Indigenous population received treatment when Miller Bay was converted to a TB sanatorium and streptomycin became available. Tragically, the hospitals became another institution in which federal policy continued the agenda of genocide – people were systematically sterilized, starved, experimented on without consent, and socially isolated from family. See Laurie Meijer Drees's book *Healing Histories: Stories from Canada's Indian Hospitals*.

28 Louisa Smith is Wa'xaid's youngest sister. She has always been in the canoe with Wa'xaid, looking out for him and her family. As matriarch, she is looked to by everyone for guidance, even those outside the family. Louisa married a Tsimshian man, Murray Smith, Algmxaa, one of the house leaders within the Gitwilgyoots tribe – House of Kelp – which is the territory known geographically as Lelu Island. See Wa'xaid's story "LNG: It Is Still Damage."

29 Diseases weren't the only arrows to come to the Kitlope in the 19th century. The Society for the Propagation of the Gospel in Foreign Parts had arrived in 1892 to "propagate" at the head of Gardner Canal. Reverend Arthur D. Price started the Kitlope Mission and school at the cannery, built by his brother, Henry. The Price Cannery, financed by the Glasgow thread company, Coats, hired villagers from Misk'usa as cannery workers and fishermen, Wa'xaid's family among them. Also in 1892, Reverend George Henry Raley and his wife Maude, who succeeded the missionary Susan Lawrence, built the first mission school in Kitamaat. See Wa'xaid's story "Elizabeth Long Memorial School: I Felt so Alone."

Two: Journey in the Magic Canoe

30 Wa'xaid wanted his story to begin with the survey markers. Starting the story with this symbol of development is logical in that a survey marker is typically the first visual clue for oral cultures – and often the only warning – that someone has arrived and laid some type of claim to their home and culture. Surveyors arrived at his family *wa'wais* at Kemano for the first time in 1874. They worked for the Canadian Pacific Railway and were laying a possible route for the railway. In 1889 the next set of survey markers marked the corner trees of the three reserves allocated to the Kitlope Indians by Peter O'Reilly. In 1906 Richard P. Bishop came up the Gardner Canal on a Canadian Hydrographic Service ship to chart the channel. Bishop walked up Kemano Bay to hunt and confirmed its waterpower potential. BC land surveyor Frank Swannell scoped out the terrain for hydro and timber in 1921. Survey markers were also laid by miners staking claims.

The most recent survey markers that Wa'xaid refers to here were put there by Eurocan Pulp & Paper Company / West Fraser in 1990. Eurocan Pulp & Paper Company was formed in the late 1960s in partnership with a Finnish national company and BC business interests. It was awarded 473,000 acres of Tree Farm Licence 41 (an area-based tenure that included the watersheds of the lower Kitimat, the Kemano, the Kildala and the Kitlope Rivers) for the princely sum of $1, as well as the Ootsa Lake region interior forests (under a Timber Supply Area, a different tenure based on volume of timber). This second tenure gave the company access to 2.7 million acres of forest for another dollar. "The somewhat imaginary authority," which Peter O'Reilly accorded to the chief, appears to have been the Canadian government, not the Haisla, since the right to allocate this timber to anyone was never legally theirs.

It was right around this time that Wa'xaid found the survey markers – those pink fluorescent tapes that herald the death knell of forests the world over. The survey markers, tied around Annie Paul's western redcedar tree where she had had raised her family on the Kitlope River, represented the first in a long chain of events.

Because of the 1987 amendments to Section 35 of the Constitution, the Haisla could pressure the government of Canada to meet their legal and constitutional obligations to protect the Haisla's "existing" oolichan fishery. The place where the survey markers were tied indicated potential log-booming grounds. This area was also the spawning grounds of oolichan, which the Haisla had a constitutional right to defend.

Today, the oolichan are gone from Kitimat River, and the only active oolichan run today is in the Kemano River watershed, the *wa-wais* owned by Wa'xaid himself. And those fish were impacted by the building of the Kenney Dam upriver in the 1950s. Rivers are affected when they are forced to run through ten miles of tunnel and eight turbines, and even minor fluctuations in water levels caused by dam flow changes are significant in the lives of small fish.

31 The Hudson's Bay Company knew it as *Kitamaat* because the Tsimshian traders called the Haisla *Kit-a-maat*, "people of the snow." The Haisla's own name for their village goes back thousands of years as *Kak-la-lee-sala*, "gravel banks" – an indication of the age of this village, being established shortly after the glaciers retreated, leaving the big banks of gravel. Likely, the difference between the spelling of the reserve name – three As: Kitamaat – and the name of the white colonial town – one A: Kitimat – started in 1897 when a sale of shares prompted a speculative railway company (to connect the Yukon goldfields) to switch its name from Kitamaat to Kitimat. In 1898 businessman C.W.D. Clifford petitioned the BC legislature for a bill to incorporate the Kitimat Railway Company. Amateur railway historian J. Gilham has speculated that this was "so that it could be found by Bankers on a map."

32 Gerald Amos comes from a long lineage of Haisla leaders. The Amos and Paul families also have a paradoxical history, intertwined with the colonization of the region. The Methodist minister, Thomas Crosby, helped convert to Christianity one of Gerald's ancestors, Charlie Amos (Wahuksgumalayou), who was born in 1853. That story is told by Elder Gordon Robinson in the local newspaper *The Northern Sentinel*, on March 6, 1958: "Charles Amos brought Christianity to Kitimat." Charlie Amos also travelled to the Kitlope to spread the gospel to Wa'xaid's family. Amos family members continue to be leaders. Gerald's father, Harry Amos, stood up for the protection of the Kitimat River all his life. Gerald stood by Wa'xaid's concern for the Kitlope from the beginning.

33 See Wa'xaid's story "Billy Hall and Bekʷus."

34 Wa'xaid refers to the union of the Eurocan company workers, which became a local chapter of the Canadian Paperworkers Union.

35 "Boston Men" is the coastal term for Americans that has survived in common usage for a good 200 years. It comes from the days when Boston traders, such as William Henry McNeill, plied the waters looking for trade in furs. The relationship of this particular group of Boston Men with Wa'xaid, Gerald and the other Haisla men continued institutionally for nearly two decades through various friendships and organizations.

36 Dr. John Pritchard was already well established in the canoe when the survey markers were found. His official title with the Haisla was researcher, and he worked with the leadership extensively on treaty rights. He arrived in Kitamaat Village in 1972, a young student of anthropology, and he stayed for 25 years. The ceremony that Wa'xaid describes in this story was made prior to the first trip to Finland that the Haisla took to meet with the Finnish-owned forestry company and stop the logging of the Kitlope.

37 The Steelhead Society of British Columbia was formed to protect this threatened member of the salmon family. Bruce Hill came to the Steelhead Society as a director. Bruce teamed up with colleague Myron Kozak and found both steelhead and survey markers in the Kitlope. One of the most publicized stories of the Kitlope is that of the apocryphal meeting of Bruce and Yvon Chouinard, the founder of Patagonia, in 1990. Hill wrote of their meeting with the Kitlope and the Haisla in Chouinard's book *Let My People Go Surfing*. Between 1990 and 1992, three separate braids of the good river were coming together in a major channel of power – the Haisla clan, the Terrace clan and the Portland clan – aligning under Wa'xaid, Louisa and Gerald's careful steering of the Magic Canoe, which they aptly named the Haisla Steering Committee. The first task of the Haisla Steering Committee and the Boston Men was to start an Ecotrust, with Gerald Amos on the board, and bring to it the full armament of research expertise in ecosystem mapping, funding and political pressure brought to bear on the provincial government and the forestry company.

38 The Haisla Steering Committee with Ecotrust also raised money to form the Haisla's own non-profit organizations, one of which was the Nanakila (Haisla for "watchman") Institute to help young people rediscover their culture through a watchman program and promote small-scale, sustainable jobs without destroying the natural capital. The other was the Haisla Nation Women's Society, which ran Rediscovery

Camps for the youth. Haisla Elders Johnnie and Bea Wilson and Hank Robertson had been seeking financial assistance since 1982 for summer camps with proper facilities, so they could teach young people how to harvest traditional foods. The name, Rediscovery Camps, was made popular by the writings of Thom Henley, who also stepped into the Magic Canoe to assist Haisla matriarchs with the summer camps.

39 The *Maple Leaf* is a century-old, 92-foot wooden schooner. Brian Falconer restored the *Maple Leaf* and brought media, environmentalists and members of the public to the Kitlope. According to Falconer, they all fell in love with the place and with the Haisla. Falconer brought trips into the Kitlope for over ten years, from the era of the West Fraser decision to the final designation of the area in 1996. The *Maple Leaf* assisted during many of Wa'xaid's battles. See the stories "Return of the G'psgolox Pole," "Kemano Completion Project: What Damage Is Going to Come of It?" and "She is Your Queen" about the plans for the Northern Gateway bitumen pipeline.

40 Dick Wells, marine historian, sailed with Brian Falconer for several trips over the years, retracing the journey found in the log of Captain George Vancouver and his crew. The section of the expedition up Gardner was part of his research.

41 Louise Barbetti is a matriarch of Kitamaat Village. She is the editor of the book *Haisla: We Are Our History*. In this document is some of her family tree, which includes her grandmother, Kate Starr, a high-born Haisla who married George Robinson, a Methodist missionary, converted by Thomas Crosby. They had a large family.

42 Captain George Vancouver's officer, Joseph Whidbey, led a shore party that reached Devastation Channel, where Gardner Canal branches off from Douglas Channel, on the evening of June 28, 1793. They spent the night at Devastation (named after HMS *Devastation*).

43 Captain George Vancouver writes of his officer Joseph Whidbey's party: "Here they were visited by eight Indians in two canoes, the first that they had seen during this expedition. The natives behaved in a very civil and friendly manner, and presented the party with two fine salmon, each weighing about 70 pounds; these were the finest and largest that had been seen during our voyage, and the Indians, after being recompensed with a small piece of iron, departed very well pleased with the exchange."

44 Gordon Robinson wrote down an account of Captain George

Vancouver's encounter with Chief Katsilanoo of the Coast Salish in English Bay in *Tales of Kitimat*. The term used for the white men is "people who can fall through boards." As Wa'xaid describes it from the deck of the schooner, *Maple Leaf*, the sailors' black hats resembled ants (some accounts further elaborate with the hatless sailors appearing to look like maggots) who slipped below the gunwales into the hold of the ship.

45 The Haisla and Ecotrust planned a reconnaissance to guide future decision making for what they called the Greater Kitlope Ecosystem, which encapsulated all 405,000 hectares. Ten Western scientists, coordinated by forest ecologist O.R. (Ray) Travers, joined Elders in the Kitlope for the first detailed scientific and cultural reconnaissance in May 1991, establishing the ecological benchmark for species of amphibians, birds, forest types, insects, mammals, mosses, plants and more. One of the scientists was Adrian Forsyth, rainforest program director for Conservation International, another organization started by the Boston Men. One of the group, John Kelson, a young climber/birder, stayed and trained youth for the Nanakila Institute.

That summer, for its 20th anniversary, Greenpeace's flagship, *Rainbow Warrior*, had scheduled a trip along the Pacific coastline to monitor the results of the two-year attempt to clean up the 11 million gallons of crude oil spilled from the *Exxon Valdez* in Prince William Sound, Alaska. The *Rainbow Warrior*'s crew also planned to look at clear-cut logging along the BC coast. It detoured into the Kitlope. The ship turned east down Gardner Canal with a delegation from Finland, Sweden, the Netherlands and the Haisla, as well as members of the study team, embracing the opportunity for media coverage and fieldwork. Following hot on their heels to catch up, BC Parks did its own two-day ground and one-day helicopter reconnaissance trips in the first week of September, led by plant ecologist Hans Roemer.

In 1993 Wa'xaid first met David Suzuki when they shared a week together aboard the HMS *World Discoverer*, conducting an educational tour of the coast, 200 years (almost to the week) after Captain Vancouver sailed into Gardner on HMS *Discovery*. Adventure Canada, an ecotourism company owned by Matt and Billy Swann, had previously run successful educational adventure tours in the area, bringing aboard scientists, activists, First Nations, artists and musicians of the region. In 1993 the Swanns launched their first West Coast educational

Forest ecologist Andy Mackinnon, above Kitlope Lake, 1993.
UNKNOWN

tour, and Wa'xaid and Suzuki were top billing. Aboard the boat were guests from across North America, and the invited speakers along the way included many of the people who would become friends and allies to the Kitlope: artists Roy Henry Vickers, Robert Davidson and Robert Bateman; musician Ian Tamblyn; scientist David Suzuki, and forest ecologists/authors Jim Pojar, Andy Mackinnon and Merve Wilkinson; and Masset Hereditary Chief Illjilwaas and Chief Pootlas from Bella Coola. Wa'xaid and Suzuki were to travel together again, for the last time, in 2004 aboard the *Spirit of Endeavor*.

Many other prominent Canadians stepped into the canoe. Ethnobotanist Wade Davis, who has written about canoe cultures around the world, was an ally although he was rumoured to have met his Waterloo when swamped by unremitting storms during his visit. The Kitlope also hosted a constant stream of international journalists who captured its magic. *Equinox Magazine* sent an expedition of scientists, a photographer and an artist to document the first Western attempt at rafting down the entire Kitlope River, starting five kilometres below the headwaters glacier – a feat that was discouraged by the Xenaksiala. Bart Robinson, the editor, had reached out to The River League guides, anxious to do the first ascent by raft; they soon regretted not heeding the Xenaksialas' advice.

Early in 1993, when former United Church minister John Cashore became the Minister of Environment, Ian Gill from the CBC thought it would be interesting to do a profile of the minister-turned-minister who was the first provincial cabinet minister to step into the Magic Canoe. Gill had heard of the Kitlope from Peter Pearse, who was on the board of Alcan at the time. Pearse told him it was a place to watch and to talk to "an outfit called Ecotrust." He did. Gill joined the media junket going up with Cashore, including *Vancouver Sun* environmental reporter Mark Hume. Little did Gill know at the time what a story he was covering and what role he would play in its unfolding. He would quit his job the following year to take on the executive director role at the newly formed Ecotrust Canada, with Gerald Amos on his board. Gill would hold that position until 2010.

46 Randy Stoltmann, climber and wilderness campaigner through his stories of the big trees of BC, had a tragic experience in the Kitlope. Best known for his *Hiking Guide to the Big Trees of British Columbia*, he fell down a crevasse on May 22, 1994, while traversing the mountains above

the Kitlope, silencing a powerful voice for ancient forests in the deep snows.

47 Heirs of fortunes like Coca Cola's (Flora) Glenn Fuller, the sons of Rockefellers, sons of Warren Buffet and son of Gordon Moore (Moore Foundation), all camped out for periods and supported the Haisla cause. Somewhere flowing along the strange current of history, from barons of resource extraction to their philanthropic children and grand-children, Wa'xaid's Magic Canoe stands ready to help a family return what an earlier generation had taken. Fuller spent some of her last days with Wa'xaid in the Kitlope. She started the Sweetgrass Foundation in 1992, dedicated to ecological health and Indigenous cultures through-out the world. Coca Cola has taken far more from Indigenous cultures around the world than it has given back, including its role in diabetes among coastal First Nations, but it is symbolic that Fuller sought out the Kitlope and Wa'xaid as "the real thing" before she passed away.

48 Ric Young is a Canadian social entrepreneur who brought his flair to the Haisla campaign. He is the Toronto-based founder of The Social Projects Studio and a world-leading architect of social-change initiatives.

49 In the next few years (through the Boston Men's connections), a suc-cession of celebrities stepped into the Magic Canoe to protect the Kitlope, including Harrison Ford, who having swashbuckled his way through jungles as Indiana Jones, donned his heavy-duty raingear for the temperate-rainforest cause. Harrison Ford sat on the board of the Rainforest Action Network, as did Bonnie Raitt, possibly the other singer mentioned by Wa'xaid as having been at the fundraiser.

50 The White Bear *Ursus americanus kermodei* is also known as the Kermode and, more recently, the Spirit Bear. It is one of 11 different sub-species of black bear, in which one bear in ten is white or cream coloured. Over a century ago, local Gitga'at hunters from Gribbell Island sent a white bear skin to Francis Kermode, curator of the then BC Provincial Museum, who sent the specimen to zoologist William T. Hornaday of the New York Zoological Society. Hornaday told Kermode that he would write up a taxonomic description and call it *Ursus alba* (white bear). Kermode wrote back saying that it should be named after him. Kermode managed to immortalize himself in the name of a bear he had never seen alive and had improperly identified, which isn't highly un-usual in the colonial tradition of naming things.

51 The late Johnny Clifton is a cherished Gitga'at Elder at Hartley Bay. The Gitga'at territory includes most of the range of the white bear, including Barnard Harbour. The Clifton family have been trading their seaweed for Kemano families' oolichan for generations.

52 The film called *Watery Vision: Is the Future Potable?*, in which Wa'xaid was featured, was a production of Deutsche Welle TV, the international arm of the German public broadcaster. Henning Hesse is listed as author of the screenplay for release in 2003.

53 When Merve Wilkinson died in 2011 at the age of 97, he was a local legend around his 136-acre Douglas-fir forest, Wildwood, near Nanaimo. Wilkinson, like Wa'xaid, was a born educator and orator and spent the last quarter-century of his life teaching his methods to visiting school and university groups at Wildwood. Wilkinson visited the Kitlope with the *Maple Leaf* and Wa'xaid visited him at Wildwood.

54 One of the early victories for the Haisla was stopping grizzly trophy hunting in their territory. The impetus for the moratorium came in the late 1980s when Elder Kenny Hall came to the Kitamaat Village Council with reports that the grizzlies of the Kitlope were disappearing; the reason was probably trophy hunting and poaching. There was little the Haisla could do until legal opportunities opened in 1990. A tipping point came when Wa'xaid encountered the grizzly hunting guide in the middle of a Rediscovery Camp. The guide, angered at the presence of children in a prime grizzly area, threatened to shoot through the kids if he saw a grizzly. It was time for the Haisla to shut down the trophy hunt. One of the objectives of the 1992 Haisla/Ecotrust Wilderness Planning Framework was to identify the potential for grizzly viewing in the Kitlope – a far more lucrative, sustainable activity than trophy hunting. Bear scientist Wayne McCrory identified the need for research on the population and the opportunities for ecotourism, and he highlighted the incompatibility of ecotourism with trophy hunting. According to John Pritchard, Bruce Hill was the catalyst for their success in this endeavour because he lent the Haisla his deep understanding of how the trophy-hunting lobby thought and worked. The Nanakila Institute generated its own data by hiring McCrory to oversee an inventory with Haisla watchmen. The inventory provided the Western evidence needed to convince the provincial government to ban trophy hunting in the Kitlope in 1994, which met with international support on one hand and threats of litigation from the trophy-hunting lobby on

the other. The Kitlope was one of the first places in BC to have trophy hunting banned, and this event helped precipitate the first-ever provincial grizzly-management strategy. It took another 23 years to shut down all trophy hunting of grizzly in the Great Bear region. The Haisla did it first.

Three: Journey of Hell

55 The flood stories are lessons in survival; some refer to the rapid flooding caused by tsunamis triggered by periodic earthquakes and others refer to the relatively slow, sea-level changes due to isostatic rebounds of the land – occurring after the weight of the glaciers came off – and the melting glacial waters. The tsunami floods occurred quickly, within hours, on roughly a 300-year rotation, and the water level rose by metres, enough to completely drown an unprepared village. The place Wa'xaid describes on the mountain called Ł'loxʷ (Thok) is about a hundred metres above the existing sea level and is directly across the canal from Kemano, where he spent time as a child. At the peak of the post-glacial flood – before the land bounced back – the sea could well have been lapping at the top of the cliff. The 'tä'ta'kwa is an osprey, and the dogfish makes sense as a food in a time of glacial upheaval. The dogfish is a shark that is well adapted to change and could take advantage during floods. Drawn to carnage, the dogfish tolerates a wide variety of habitats with big ranges of salinity and depth, so it does well in brackish waters. The dogfish could also easily illustrate a lesson in conservation, as it is vulnerable to overfishing. The northern spiny dogfish takes up to 35 years to mature, has the longest gestation of any invertebrate (up to two years) and produces small litters of maybe half a dozen pups. Humans are the dogfish's main predator, especially the humans who engage in the type of industrial fishing that wipes out schools of an entire age class. The dogfish is protected internationally, but Canada has done little to protect it. The flood story illustrated through the Kemano pole (explained by Wa'xaid in his story "Eighty per cent Industry, 20 per cent Natural Causes") elevates the dogfish to a place on a totem pole that reminds one to be mindful.

His granny also mentions the floods occurring from earthquakes. In the last 20 years, the study of paleotsunamis has thrown some Western-scientific light on cycles well known to coastal peoples. When you dig a pit in a bog whose soil profile stretches back in time, you see slim layers of light tsunami-deposited sands interspersed between the thick, dark, organic soils. Tsunamis turn coastal bogs into striped storybooks. We know that tsunamis have likely occurred dozens of times since the glaciers retreated. The most recent tsunami was an eight-metre wave in Douglas Channel causing severe damage to port facilities in Kitimat on April 27, 1975. The flood stories include people getting in a canoe and getting out to sea for safety – advice that is still essential today.

The rivers also flood seasonally after deluges, rising metres within hours. Being caught on a river in a flood event can be terrifying, and drowning is an ever-present fear on the river. The teachings about the arrival of death coming to the door were some that prepared Wa'xaid for when the Indian agent came knocking at his family's door the first time in 1937.

56 With the influenza epidemic barely past, Duncan Campbell Scott, deputy minister of Indian Affairs, told the Special Committee of the House of Commons Investigating the Indian Act Amendments of 1920 that "our object is to continue until there is not a single Indian in Canada that has been absorbed into the body politic" (see Truth and Reconciliation Commission of Canada [TRC], *Honouring the Truth, Reconciling for the Future: Summary of the Final Report of the Truth and Reconciliation Commission of Canada*, volume 1, 2015, p. 3). The policy to not absorb but eradicate a culture was obvious as "the mere presence of indigenous people in these newly colonized lands blocked settler access to the land" (see TRC, volume 1, 2015, p. 46). The Indian Act was further amended to make it illegal to withhold children between seven and 15 from attending the residential schools. In Section 10, the act holds: "Every Indian child between the ages of seven and fifteen years who is physically able shall attend such day, industrial or boarding school as may be designated by the Superintendent General for the full periods during which such school is open each year."

Alberni, Kitamaat and Port Simpson schools, started by the early missionaries in the 1870–1890s, all became the responsibility of the United Church of Canada under the care of the Women's Missionary Society in the early 1920s, when they started receiving grants per student from the federal government. By 1930 there were 80 residential schools across the country, and any guardian of a child who withheld that child from going to school would be sent to jail. This was the world Wa'xaid was born into in 1931. At the age of six, his father was forced to bring him down from Kemano to his first compulsory residential school, the Elizabeth Long Memorial Home (founded in 1896) in Kitamaat. Wa'xaid had no idea that his family would be jailed if his father had not enrolled him.

57 Hiding Wa'xaid from 1938 to 1941 was probably only possible because of the shortage of available government representatives with the onset of the war. It was illegal to hide him. His grandparents, Johnnie and Annie Paul, were obviously able to keep one of their small grandsons away from the Indian agent's eyes for a few years as they moved between their trapline and oolichan camp in the Kemano area, their house on the Kitlope River, and other seasonal camps.

One of the Methodist ministers who was welcomed to the Kitlope by the Paul family was Dr. Peter Kelly, a Haida leader who was an ardent activist for First Nations. In Eric Jamieson's book, *The Native Voice*, Dr. Kelly is described as a "humble diplomat and stood fast by his beliefs, even at times setting himself against the very church that employed him" (p. 43). Paul Tennant, in *Aboriginal Peoples and Politics: The Indian Land Question in BC*, writes that in 1911 Kelly led Allied Tribes for BC, the first organization to "move the land claims through the court system to the Judicial Committee." He later led the Native Brotherhood, which was founded the year Wa'xaid was born.

58 Wa'xaid's story of his childhood is understandably linked to devil's club and its beautiful fragrance. Devil's club, *'wi¹qas* (a-WEE-q'us), grows throughout the wetter lowland areas of the valleys. Its common English name comes from Christian colonizers who noticed that when you walk through the bush in the winter, the plant looks like a gnarly, devilish club on a long, spiny handle. The white spikes of the plant's flowers ripen into deep red berries by late summer, just like those of its cousin ginseng; both are highly important medicinal plants embraced by the East and the West. Every part of the plant has some medicinal or ceremonial purpose; it is a first-aid kit growing in the forest, pointing to life-giving water and immune-boosting properties. It may well have been the tonic that kept Wa'xaid alive through a century of epidemics.

59 Wa'xaid was transported over a thousand kilometres to the head of Alberni Inlet in central Vancouver Island. He arrived at an imposing new brick building on the Somass River that had just been built to replace the school that had burned down. It was the third to burn down, probably not by accident. He described it as a prison, which it indeed

resembled with its square, fortress-like appearance and small windows. Today, there is nothing left of the school, just a patch of forest near the Tseshaht Reserve. Upon his arrival, Wa'xaid was registered as #126 in the Quarterly Returns, the official documents sent to Ottawa with the children's attendance that triggered the payment of the annual fee per student to the United Church. The Quarterly Returns records: his arrival on September 1941; that he is from the Kemano tribe; that he is 11 years old; and that he is placed in Grade 4 for F&G (Farming and Gardening) trade. His attendance was the maximum number of days for the quarter. Since Wa'xaid did not leave the school for four years, his attendance was 100 per cent. The remarks about him on the far column of the report state, "Satisfactory progress."

Andrew Paull, and Indigenous leader of the Allied Tribes of BC and later the Native Brotherhood, was an early critic of the residential schools. He drew attention to the abuse of a staff member at Alberni, who he wrote on August 21, 1922, "'unmercifully whips the boys on their back' as well as kicking them, hitting them with fists, and choking them." (See "Children Remembered," http://thechildrenremembered.ca/school-locations/alberni/#ftn31.) Just prior to Wa'xaid arriving, a school inspector for Ahousat, Gerald H. Barry, complained in his "Report on Ahousat Indian Residential School" (March 24, 1936) that "[c]hildren have come here from Alberni Indian Residential School, where every member of the Staff carried a strap….These children have never learned how to work without punishments." (See RG10, vol. 6430, file 876-6, pt. 1, Library and Archives Canada.) Documentation of life in Alberni residential school during the Second World War is limited.

60 R.C. Scott was a Methodist minister who was the principal of Alberni during Wa'xaid's time there. He was appointed by the United Church, but he was paid by the Department of Indian Affairs. In his memoir, *My Captain Oliver: A Story of Two Missionaries on the British Columbia Coast*, Scott writes, "After I went to Alberni Residential School as principal in 1940, I had within a year or two a better idea of what was actually wrong with these people" (p. 180). What was "wrong," apparently, was the Elders. "There is another very powerful reason why such people do not make any outward objection to the carrying on of old customs. These old people who have taken over the direction of affairs in the life of the

Reserves have their own way of forcing compliance and cooperation. Sometimes their methods are heartless and cruel" (p. 182).

Scott's personal journal includes entries about his interactions with the students at the school.

April 29th, 1941 – This has been a trying time, but I cannot feel that a mistake has been made in my coming here. I do seem to be out of place in my methods perhaps, and I shall have to overhaul them, and perhaps revise them.

August 3, 1942 – Buddy Hamilton came to the office and said he wanted to see Mr. Grantham before me. His plaint was that the boy in question, Arthur Pearson, had been crying and Buddy took this as an evidence of his being unkindly treated. The fact was that money had been given the boy, and he wanted to go to the store without permission. I felt "riled" at Buddy, and told him what he and the other boys were doing in making it hard to enforce discipline and that unless they changed and fell in line with me, and the school programme, they would have to stay away together. This incident shows the "uppishness" and insolence of these young fellows. To think they have the right to come to the office and interfere, or criticize the member of staff! Well, that seems the limit. I am tempted to just shut down, and keep them out for good, but here again, that would mean that these boys would stay on their own side of the fence and make as much, if not more trouble than ever.

61 Sir John A. Macdonald made these remarks in the House of Commons in 1883, which were to direct policy on Indian affairs in Canada for the next century: "He [the Indian] is simply a savage who can read and write. It has been strongly pressed on myself, as the head of the Department, that Indian children should be withdrawn as much as possible from the parental influence, and the only way to do that would be to put them in central training industrial schools where they will acquire the habits and modes of thought of white men" (See Truth and Reconciliation Commission of Canada, *Honouring the Truth, Reconciling for the Future: Summary of the Final Report of the Truth and Reconciliation Commission of Canada*, volume 1, 2015, p. 2).

62 Reggie Wilson appears in the Quarterly Returns as student #2. On June 30, 1943, the remarks are uncharacteristically effusive: "Excellent pupil. Passed first in High School Entrance Class." According to Isobel

McFadden's accounts of life in the schools, *Living by Bells: A Story of Five Indian Schools 1874–1970*, 1970, the local Indian agents and school inspectors had blocked promising students from even taking the entrance exams during principal Mr. P. Pitt's era at the school. The inspector was said to have claimed: "most Indians want to go back to their reserves anyway." Reggie Wilson appears to have broken through one glass ceiling – an opportunity to take the exam. There still lay ahead the challenge of getting into high school, which Wa'xaid recalls was not an opportunity offered.

63 All that appears in the Quarterly Returns about these students are their names, numbers and attendance records, with very limited comments on progress: Reggie Wilson, #2; Art Pearson, #134; Larry King, #146; Percy Mack, #149; brother Douglas Paul, #150; cousin Charlie Shaw, #165; Russell Ross, #169; cousin Crosby Smith, #192. These men went on to become leaders in their communities and shared many of the same arrows. The list of leaders from this intake extends well beyond Wa'xaid's connections too. In *Living by Bells: A Story of Five Indian Schools 1874–1970*, Isobel McFadden writes about an evening spent with Jim Manly, a United Church minister who was at the forefront of collecting testimonies from survivors of the schools. In her book, McFadden paraphrases one of the voices Manly recorded: "when Indians named the men and women and young people who were leaders in the communities and leaders in the current Indian movements, almost all had been students in these same church schools. In spite of the miseries, the education had prepared them to devise their ideas for the betterment of their people and to deal with problems." McFadden and Wa'xaid might disagree on what "education" refers to, but there is no doubt that those who survived were educated in survival and resilience.

64 Reverend A.E. Caldwell took over the school in 1944, and one important improvement he may have engineered (it only receives a footnote by the commissioner) is the resignation of a Mr. R.E. Allen, possibly the same man named by Wa'xaid as "his tormentor." No other reference to him in any United Church or government documents could be found, nor what happened to him. Wa'xaid remembers one staff member who was "a good guy," Edward Peak.

65 Two years after Wa'xaid left Alberni, Arthur Henry Plint took over as the boys' night supervisor at Alberni, a position of power that Plint abused for the next 20 years. Vincent Paul was incarcerated in the school

sometime during the same year Plint arrived. He ran away with three others from Alberni, all of whom got caught by the police. Vincent Paul was one of the first students to escape recapture by the RCMP. He was essentially an outlaw for his teenage years, then he worked for a fisherman. He was only 26 when he died. Alberni survivors from between 1948 and 1968 testified about the physical and sexual abuse they suffered during the landmark Willie Blackwater criminal and civil court cases beginning in the mid-1990s (there were originally 26 survivors/witnesses). These were the first court cases to alert Canadians to the abuse going on in residential schools across Canada. If Vincent had lived to testify, he might well have been one of the witnesses. In 1995 Arthur Henry Plint was charged with 18 counts of sexual assault between 1948 and 1968. The landmark Blackwater case would reveal levels of abuse that prompted BC Supreme Court Justice Douglas Hogarth to declare in the sentencing of Arthur Plint in 1995 that the Indian residential school system "was nothing but a form of institutionalized pedophilia" (See *Macleans Magazine*, 3 April 1995). In 2003 Donald Bruce Haddock, another member of staff, pleaded guilty to four counts of indecent assault between 1948 and 1954.

66 Stories of abuse at Alberni during Wa'xaid's time through the war years only came to light during the Truth and Reconciliation Commission's work in 2013, with the testimony of former students like Wa'xaid. The post-war years were exposed in 1995 with the testimonies presented in the Willie Blackwater criminal (and later civil) court cases. Willie Blackwater was a student at Alberni a few years after Wa'xaid left. An investigation of schools by the RCMP was initiated across BC, but by then there was already a long institutional foundation for the violence. Blackwater was the first survivor to step forward and not just initiate the criminal charges, which Plint pleaded guilty to during his trial, but to take it further into the civil courts, right up until 2005, to determine who was responsible for the institutionalized violence: the federal government or the United Church?

According to Reverend Brian Thorpe, Minister Emeritus of Ryerson United Church, who worked on the residential school file from 1994 onwards, there was a marked difference in the day-to-day involvement of the federal government in the management of the schools before and after the Second World War. A detailed analysis of who was responsible for the abuses of the residential schools was put before the courts in the

Blackwater civil court case against the federal government, which according to Thorpe became "a debate around the question of apportion of responsibility" (Personal communication with Thorpe, 29 Nov. 2016). At the end of the Blackwater case, which went through two courts of appeal, the Supreme Court of Canada concluded that federal government had 75 per cent of the responsibility, and the United Church 25. Thorpe states, "There are those in the United Church who still argue that we had no real act to play... but the reality is that the United Church still attached its name to the school. It still took incredible pride in the history of the school and did nothing to challenge the existence of the school. For those reasons alone, the church has to bear a responsibility."

When I spoke with him in 2016, Thorpe's analysis was:

> From the government's perspective, their hope was that the church could shoulder the responsibility which from a purely political point of view you can understand. The problem is that it separates the residential school process from colonization. Sadly, in the public mind, I think it is still a very strong dimension that somehow the residential schools are a stand alone experience – a tragic period in history – but people don't make the connection with all the other processes of colonization. The loss of land, the loss of resources, all of those that are integrally tied together and that is why it is important that the whole notion of residential schools is understood as a Canadian project. The problem is when the churches say that, it can be easily seen as trying to shuffle off your responsibility. I think it is still such a dominant unexamined thread throughout the Canadian psyche and through the Christian church psyche. People can understand sexual abuse and be horrified by it but the racism that lies at the centre of it is still unacknowledged.

67 Sometime after Wa'xaid was released from Alberni Indian Residential School, he got a job washing dishes on a fishing boat. The fishing boat arrived at the southernmost *wa'wais* of the Haisla people, Butedale or Cedixs. Cedixs refers in the Haisla language to the state of your stomach after eating too many thimble- and salmonberries, a bounty of which Cedixs offered. The cannery was officially named Butedale on the maps in 1946, after the third Earl of Bute, John Stuart, of Scotland, who was both a botanist and a prime minister of Britain. His knowledge of the *Rubus* genus of the berries would undoubtedly have exceeded

his knowledge of the place, never having been there. He died in 1792, the year his fellow countryman Alexander Mackenzie became the first European to cross the continent to the West Coast, finishing his journey along the well-travelled grease highway.

Butedale was once one of the largest canneries on the coast, with its own small hydroelectric generating plant. The town, now a western ghost town, once boasted a packinghouse, icehouse, herring-oil reduction plant and tanks, general store and school for a town of 400 people. The Indian bunkhouses were just above the little creek that turns into a roaring torrent in the winter. They were the first to get washed out into the ocean. Each ethnic group working at Butedale – Chinese, Japanese and Indigenous – lived in different bunkhouses. The closer to the white manager's home, the higher the status. The Indians were always the farthest away.

In 1946 Wa'xaid was 15 years old. Many of his family members were dead, dying, in residential school, at Indian hospitals or escaping them. He never heard from or spoke to any member of his family in those four years. They didn't even know where he was. Some sense of the isolation of Kitamaat Village that year is captured in an article written by Reverend Bunt during his tour of the Indian missions. "By the next evening we had reached Kitamaat which is without a missionary, without a telephone or telegraph, and without a nurse. The nearest doctor is over 150 miles distant and the nearest telephone 75 miles away."(See W.P. Bunt, "President and Superintendent Tours Indian Missions," in *Western Recorder*, 21 (February 1946): 2).

68 There are several Xenaksiala and Haisla stories about the perils of mistreating frogs. Death is the usual consequence of disrespecting nature. One frog story, which belongs to the Hall family, is about a girl who married a frog, giving birth to the frog families. It all takes place in a village on an island in the Kitlope River, just upriver from where Wa'xaid grew up. Contemporary Western attitudes are predominantly indifferent to amphibious relatives; but some scientists are like John Kelson, a Western scientist who got into the Magic Canoe and helped Nanakila do a survey of the amphibians of the Kitlope in 1992. It turns out that Haisla territory is one of the few places in the world where amphibians don't appear to be dying out. As of this writing, 64 per cent of frog and toad species in BC are listed as species of concern. Even the western toad is experiencing sharp population declines in the south, from

habitat destruction and deadly fungal diseases brought in by humans. Not surprisingly, the Kitlope watershed is vitally important globally, not only because of the large, unmodified area but because the remoteness means there are fewer chances for deadly pathogens like introduced fungal diseases to arrive with humans.

69 In May 1947, Wa'xaid's uncle, Guy Williams, Haida leader and Methodist minister, Dr. Peter Kelly, and Chief William Scow (then president of the Native Brotherhood of BC) used their own money and resources to travel to Ottawa, representing the "unaffiliated First Nations people of the province" (see Eric Jamieson, *The Native Voice*, 2016, p. 81) to speak to the Special Joint Committee of the Senate and House of Commons looking into revisions to the Indian Act. They came with optimism and brought arguments on bringing equity for Native people with respect to political representation, education, medical care, access to fish, pensions and so on, including, as always, treaty rights. At that meeting, Peter Kelly spoke about segregation and specifically used the example of Prince Rupert's movie theatre in which "the effect, psychologically, is damaging. Treatment such as that breeds an inferiority complex....They have been browbeaten to a point where they simply accept those things. I mean to say that personal dignity, somehow, can be just beaten down until it is broken down" (see Guy Williams, *The Native Voice Newsletter*, May 1947, p. 11). It may well have been Wa'xaid's experience that precipitated Kelly using this example, or Haida member Jane Adams, daughter of the founder of the Native Brotherhood of BC, Alfred Adams, who was asked to move and refused. She wasn't jailed but expressed having felt deep humiliation. The concerns raised by the BC delegates were ignored, once again.

70 Asian immigrants faced many of the same prejudices that First Nations people experienced in Prince Rupert. Places like the Grand Café and the West End Café offered friendship, food and warmth to the non-white community. When Wa'xaid walked in to the West End Café after 30 years of being away, the waitress recognized him and brought him a coffee with three sugars without having to ask.

71 Wa'xaid's uncle, Guy Williams, wrote of the origins of the Native Brotherhood in *The Native Voice* in 1960:

> The efforts and the cause of a once noble race seemed altogether lost until one day a Haida Chief and Tsimshian noblemen gathered together in the embers and coals of the fires of the beaten

Allied Tribes of BC. Then was born the Native Brotherhood of BC. Now after 17 years this organization is recognized as the largest and most democratic Native organization in Canada and has continually strived for a change of status and for the betterment of existing conditions among the natives. (p. 5)

The Native Brotherhood (and the Native Sisterhood) has had powerful leadership throughout its nearly 90-year history. The organizations grew out of earlier efforts with the Allied Tribes of BC. The first leaders were thoughtful men, educated in both cultures, like Reverend Peter Kelly (Haida Gwaii), Chief Andy Paull (Xwechtaal) (Squamish Nation), and Chief William Scow (Gla-Whay-Agliss) (Kwie-kwa-sutineuk Nation). Since then, the Native Brotherhood has sent delegation after delegation to Ottawa and been consistently ignored.

Wa'xaid also mentions Heber Maitland, whose contributions are legion. One of the many letters that Maitland penned over the years is an example of his contributions. In 1978 BC Premier Bill Vander Zalm came up with a "solution to the problem of young Natives living in the slums of Vancouver" – "Ship Indians to Reserve" (see *The Province*, 17 June 1978, p. 4). Mr. Vander Zalm was also the creator of an amusement park called Fantasy Gardens. Here is part of Maitland's response to the Honourable Allan Williams regarding that proposal: "Unfortunately, Mr. Vander Zalm's quick and easy solution will change nothing for the Minister has been poorly advised and has mistaken cause and effect. Native people are not drawn to the city simply for 'bright lights and excitement' that is casually insulting and shows a deep ignorance of Indians and conditions that afflict them....What draws Native people south is desperation, lack of opportunity and lack of hope..." (see Maitland correspondence to Hon. L. Allan Williams, Minister of Labour, 20 June 1978, in Iona Campagnolo Fonds, UNBC Archives, 2009.6.13.17.063 Indian and Northern Affairs/Indian Bands, Councils and Reserves/Kitamaat).

72 Wa'xaid's uncle was one of the last canoe makers of the Kitlope. He never got to pass the skill on to his nephew. Just when Wa'xaid would have been starting his training in earnest, he was taken away to residential school. That interruption of training, repeated in village after village, killed the canoe culture. At the turn of the century, there were about 10,000 canoes on the coast, but by 1950, most of them were rotting in the forest and few new ones were being made (see "Northwest Coast

Canoes," http://www.sfu.ca/brc/art_architecture/canoes.html). The other big factor, of course, was mechanization. Ole Evinrude, who invented the small outboard motor, was a Norwegian who knew fjords and the advantages of a motor. The outboards, which started at 1 and 2 HP, won hands down over paddling, but the cost to Indigenous peoples meant entering the cash economy. During the Depression, with low fish prices and high gas prices, paddles still held their own. But, by 1954, with its relatively low price, the 5.5 Evinrude CD model and the light metal boats left the canoe in a slow eddy.

The final requirement for a vibrant canoe culture lies in the supply of huge western redcedars. A tree needs to be at least 500 years old and 2 metres in diameter at the butt to be big enough to carve into a canoe. Western redcedar was hard hit by industrial logging up and down the coast, especially in the last 50 years as demand escalated. The tree's increasing scarcity has been a critical concern in places like Haida Gwaii, where cultural revitalization relies on enabling cedars to grow to the size and maturity required for canoe craft. The huge western redcedars of the Kitlope were another critical factor in the decision to ensure the Kitlope was protected from industrial logging. No trees means no canoes, and so no canoe culture to revitalize. One of the first projects of the Nanakila Institute was starting the offshoot organization the Haisla Canoe Society, to build a canoe with the renaissance of canoe culture in 1986.

73 Johnny Paul's walk to a Native Brotherhood meeting sometime in the 1930s along the Xesdu'wäxd [Huschduwasch] grease trail is just one of hundreds of journeys taken by different members of the early brotherhood, who were scattered over a huge province with few modern transportation routes. To share their collective voice required a dedication that is hardly imaginable today. It took Johnny Paul at least a week, travelling over very rugged country and making difficult river crossings, to make the meeting. The refusal by government to listen to the reasonable requests of the Native Brotherhood is another dismal chapter in the history of Canadian colonialism – a chapter that has not ended.

The grease trail Johnny Paul followed had been largely neglected since the turn of the 19th century. Prior to colonization, the trails formed a major transportation network – a web of trading routes leading from the half-dozen oolichan rivers of the coast to the interior. They were maintained by coastal traders moving oolichan oil east and interior traders moving goods (obsidian, smoked moose, moose hides, sheep, goat horn, wool and furs) west. The Kemano trail went over the pass to Tahtsa Lake, and the Kitlope had a second trail that went south to the Nuxalk at Dean Inlet. The Kitlope families like the Pauls traded just north of one of the five Nuxalk trails that Alexander Mackenzie used in July 1793 during the "first" east–west crossing of North America. He was travelling with a party of five Nuxalk families to Bella Coola. At that time, elaborate bridges crossed the rivers, and villages marked stops along the way.

74 When Wa'xaid was brought, unconscious, by his cousin Crosby Smith (named by the missionaries after the reverend Thomas Crosby) into Kemano's wharf in 1951, a fully paved road went 20 kilometres up to the Kemano construction camp. Close to 2,500 single men and 44 families were living there to build the tunnel through Mount Dubose. The road that followed Wa'xaid's family's trapline was named Horetzky – after the surveyor, Charles Horetzky – and continued to Tahtsa Lake. Wa'xaid was lucky that Kemano had a helicopter, as he had probably lost enough blood to be close to dying when they flew him to the Miller Bay Indian Hospital. The chopper pilots were some of the most skilled in the world, having to negotiate the thermal winds so common in the mountains. He was also lucky he got the man Wa'xaid calls Dr. Mack. (There is no "Dr. Mack" in the BC Directory for Prince Rupert in 1951, but there is a Dr. G.J. Macdonald listed as an employee at Miller Bay Indian Hospital.) Wa'xaid remembers him as a skilled doctor, trained in the air force to handle war injuries, who reconstructed his badly mangled hand at a time when institutional discrimination was the norm.

Grey wolves in the Kitlope have a distinctive reddish hue to their coats and a mostly marine diet. In the past, coastal wolves were split into three coastal subspecies. Recent studies confirm that they are a haplotype, which means that the genetic profile of these wolves varies from the ones in the interior. They are an important population because wolves have been extirpated from southern Canada, and the coastal populations are restricted to remote, roadless places like the Kitlope. The genetic variation suggests that these wolves might well have been isolated from their cousins 360,000 years ago, during the last glaciation. When you see wolves in the Kitlope, you usually see them swimming: in rivers as they fish for salmon, to rocky islets after seals, or across channels after deer, which regularly outswim them. It makes sense that Wa'xaid was called Wolf with One Paw. Wolves caught in traps are known to chew off their trapped paw and adapt to a life with only one paw in front or back. In the last 20 years, the wolves in the Great Bear Rainforest have become some of the most studied and secure populations of wolves on Earth. The Xenaksiala, the human relations, have been less fortunate. After smallpox, the Wolf Clan died out, the names dying with the people.

75 The Pearson brothers from Haida Gwaii were at Alberni with Wa'xaid. Leonard Pearson was #133 and Art was #134. Missionary R.C. Scott mentions Art in his diaries as a boy with "uppishness." Cumshewa Inlet was the name that surveyor G.M. Dawson settled on after a period of unsuccessfully recording the Haida name, Hlk̲'inul. It is the inlet that lies between Moresby and Louise Island. The trees were so huge and numerous that the only railway ever built on Haida Gwaii was to haul timber from the camps to the inlet. When the Second World War hit, there was a big push to find spruce for airplanes, hence the naming of the Crown corporation, Aero. After the war, Aero was bought out by the Powell River Company, which employed Wa'xaid as a longshoreman to bundle logs into Davis rafts, a type of log boom designed in 1911 by a Port Renfrew logger, G.G. Davis. They were bundles of up to a million board feet of timber, 250 feet long, 60 feet wide and 30 feet deep. They were tied and secured through a system of weaving wire ropes though the logs, which made the bundles resilient to stormy sea conditions. There are not enough trees anymore to make those kinds of Davis bundles, unless, of course, the government opens places like the Kitlope for logging.

76 Logger/poet Hibby Grens of Cumshewa also refers to Panicky Bell in his poem, "Logger Splice Away Back When":

Viv Williams, Art Holland and Panicky Bell,

I logged with them as my poems tell,

Logger splice here's how it goes,

Tuck 1 and 2 and 3 and 4,

Now No. 5 takes its first dive,

Then No. 6 does its first trix,

Followed again by No. 1,

Continue like this and soon you're done.

77 Kitimat to Terrace was once a 75-kilometre-long, 10-kilometre-wide glacial highway. The kilometre-high glacier ploughed a swath, then it retreated, leaving a highly productive floodplain through which the Kitimat River ran and trees grew. On May 7, 1952, according to *Canadian Hansard*, Lionel Chevrier, federal minister of Transport, stood up in Parliament to announce to Canadians a plan to construct a transit corridor to access the valley's "21 billion feet of accessible timber" and move aluminum to the interior railway node of Terrace, where it could be dispersed across Canada. The railway came first and the highway quickly after. Wa'xaid's job was servicing the surveyors who moved through the country by riverboat.

The flash flood of the Kitimat Valley that swamped Wa'xaid was also mentioned in a letter written on February 1, 1977, by Milton Weber, superintendent and member of the management committee for Kitimat Construction, to Iona Campagnolo: "At 9 p.m. the crew were bedded down in summer tents. Suddenly the temperatures of the atmosphere rose a great deal and in less than an hour the water in the river rose 19 feet or more. The crew in night attire took plotting charts etc. and crawled up the trees to avoid being drowned. By morning the people at Kitimat Construction Camp observed gear and other material of the surveyors floating down the river." Press reports state that there were big floods and that Williams Creek, the *wa 'wais* of Wa'xaid's wife Mae Williams, flooded the Lakelse Road that Wa'xaid eventually walked out on.

78 The award Wa'xaid mentions is the Hero of the Planet award from the Rainforest Action Network (RAN) in San Francisco. Wa'xaid was an obvious recipient for this award by an organization that "preserves forests, protects climate and upholds human rights by challenging corporate power." The Kitlope was one of the regions RAN helped with the "challenging corporate power" piece. Bruce Hill and Ian Gill both remember the gala evening at Golden Gate Park in 1994 when Wa'xaid accepted his award, because they went with him. In Bruce Hill's words: "He was really reluctant to go." When Bruce asked why, Wa'xaid told him that he thought he was going to get stopped at the border because of his old gambling spree and jail sentence in Alaska. There weren't any problems at the border, though, and Wa'xaid met Indigenous leaders from the Amazon there.

79 One of the few attractions at Butedale for Wa'xaid was a young woman,

Marguerite Demers. After the Second World War, Marguerite's parents Dorothy (Dot) and Paul Demers had run a fish camp at Crab River in Gardner Canal and met many of the Kitlope families who stopped in to sell fish or buy gas and ice. The Paul family was one of them. When I spoke with Marguerite on January 17, 2017, she recalled, "Johnnie [Paul, Wa'xaid's grandfather] would come in, while Mom was working and Dad was out on the fish boat, and he would tell her stories about the Kitlope. It is too bad she isn't alive to ask her. It was that connection that probably led to Wa'xaid coming over to visit."

Marguerite's parents had both been cooks in the air force during the war. Her father had come out to Coal Harbour. After being discharged, they decided to make their way fishing on the coast. According to Marguerite, "My father knew nothing about fishing." She was born in 1947 and grew up first at Crab River and later at Whisky Cove, where her parents homesteaded in a bay across the channel from Butedale – 3.5 miles south. Her childhood became increasingly difficult. Her father had gone though a war and a family before his current one and he began drinking. He had trained as a lightweight spar boxer.

The Haisla women frequently dropped by, including Annie Paul, Wa'xaid's grandmother. As Marguerite told me, "She would sit there and laugh with Mom and drink her tea." Marguerite's best friends were Haisla girls Cecelia Grant and Liza Nyce. "They were daughters number 2 and 3." The Demers had few other visitors; occasional missionaries stopped by on the *Thomas Crosby* mission boat. Marguerite helped her father trap on his trapline and could hunt and fish like any boy: "I don't think my dad thought I was a girl until I had that baby." Wa'xaid "fell into our lives as so many young people came and went. We had a 'thing' – very short term." By this time, Paul Demers' addiction had spread to barbiturates. Marguerite was dealing with an increasingly traumatized father. During an event involving the RCMP and firearms, her mother had a breakdown and fled by rowboat with the children to Butedale to meet the *Thomas Crosby* which took them to refuge in a Prince Rupert safe house – the United Church Friendship House. When they returned to Whisky Cove, her father had the two dogs put down. Then, her best friend Cecelia Grant (after whom she named the baby) was killed in a car accident. That was the environment in which 15-year-old Marguerite became pregnant in the autumn of 1962. "The last time I saw Wa'xaid, I remember there was chum salmon still going up the creek."

She thought he was heading back to Kitamaat for the winter. She never told him she was pregnant.

The delivery was not straightforward; her water broke, and she went into hard labour right away. He father had attended the delivery of his previous children so, "I remember him rolling up his sleeves. He made some disparaging remarks about Wa'xaid. Her father went into Butedale to get some help. "I wasn't getting anywhere so they got an emergency airlift the next day. It was really touch and go. I can remember Mom being called in, crying and asking if I was going to make it. The ministry was there to get the baby and the signatures for adoption. I wasn't even out of the anaesthetic before they asked me to sign." It was a forceps delivery, which caused hemorrhaging. In the medical records for the adoption, it says it was a normal birth. She was allowed no visitors. The baby was put at the back of the nursery and covered from view, as she was not permitted to see her. "I think the nurse felt sorry for me because I came out of the anesthetic and I heard this baby crying. When I glanced over the side, the nurse showed me a baby. She made eye contact with me and she stopped crying."

Before her mother took the family away for good in August 1963, Marguerite believes she saw Wa'xaid at Butedale in front of the cold storage. "I just told him that he had a daughter and she was put up for adoption. My life was so piecemeal back then, because the family was in disruption, everything was crashing the year Cecelia was born … 63 – other than her, there was nothing good about it." Her memories of Cecil being told to leave Butedale are also vague. "I didn't care about anything." Her mother took her and her brother first back to Ottawa and then to Vancouver. Marguerite Demers started drinking and didn't stop until friends helped her back onto her feet 18 months later. She never stopped looking for her daughter.

80 Clara Thompson, Wa'xaid's mother, was in the Eagle Clan. She married Thomas Paul, and they had 11 children before he died of TB. Ten of them were sent to residential school and one to Indian hospital. Bald eagles are as much a part of the Kitlope as the huge Sitka spruce root balls upon which they perch in full view of the village. They are always waiting for something to swim up the river and wash up on the beach. The eagles are ever-present relatives in the Kitlope, faithful to their nest sites.

81 The seeds for the extraordinary coincidence of the meeting of the

two fathers, birth and adopted, of Cecelia Cashore, Wa'xaid and John Cashore (in his later capacity as minister of Environment), began in the tiny northern community of Port Simpson or Lax Kw'alaams when the baby was delivered to the Cashores. John Cashore was newly ordained and taking up the reins of the United Church in this Tsimshian village. The other extraordinary coincidence was Louisa and Murray Smith being friends with the Cashores without knowing that the Cashores' adopted baby was in fact Louisa's niece.

82 Where the Tulsequah enters the Taku River are rich seams of copper, lead, silver and gold that were first exposed to prospectors who staked Tulsequah Chief Mine in 1925. Cominco started mining underground in earnest in 1951, working the mine for six years before markets and seams dried up. Wa'xaid must have been at the site just after it closed to full production. Hundreds of men would have moved the rock up from the ground to a processing site right on the banks of the Tulsequah. The ore was crushed and mixed with water and cyanide, creating acid tailings ponds that continue to pour into the Taku today.

Xenaksiala Elder the late Gordon Robertson told Emmon Bach, the linguist, a story about a Haisla gambler in the old days who gambled so much that he lost everything: "his own house and his canoe and winter food and his freedom and the freedom of this wife and children, and he lost his little finger." The resolution for the gambler is to cleanse and strengthen with devil's club. "Nobody knew that the devil's club was a powerful medicine until the plant itself came alive."(See Louise Barbetti, ed., *We Are Our History*, June 21, 2005.) The story goes that devil's club comes alive and asks the man what happened to him, and then the plant instructs the gambler to go and wash himself down and chew the bark to cleanse himself. It gives him the ability to see through his hands to the bones, and he wins everything back. Wa'xaid followed the instructions to a tee. Everything came back to him too, except his missing fingers. The BC government was not so lucky. The Tulsequah Chief Mine's toxic leaching continues to haunt politicians, and Alaskan First Nations continue to call on BC to clean the mess up, over 60 years later.

83 The Oxford Group has almost been forgotten, but it had a profound impact on the people of the coast. The story of its formation begins in a street-side church in Philadelphia in 1908 with a young social worker called Frank Buchman. He had started a hospice for young men off the streets with a garden allotment, when the church cut his budget. After

resigning, he ended up at Oxford University where he formed a spiritual group that aimed at fellowship with the goals of love, purity, honesty and unselfishness. The movement caught on all over the world and attracted men like Bill W. (William Griffith Wilson), Ebby T. (Ebby Thacher), Rowland H. (Rowland Hazard) and Dr. Bob S. (Robert Holbrook Smith), who went on to start Alcoholics Anonymous (AA) on the same principles. Ebby T. was a chronic drunk in Vermont and had been thrown into prison. Rowland H. (who had been taught by Carl Jung) and two other Oxford Group followers bailed him out. The rescued Ebby T. went on to save his childhood friend Bill W., through the Oxford Group tenets: "We admit we were licked. We got honest with ourselves. We talked it over with one another. We made amends to those who we had harmed" (See "Oxford Group Connection," *History of Alcoholics Anonymous*, silkworth.net). Bill W. is the acknowledged founder of AA and a continuing influence on Wa'xaid's healing.

84 Two of the most colourful coastal members of AA's prototype, the Oxford Group (it later became Moral Re-Armament), were Rollo and Kay Boas. Rollo Boas was the son of the "adopted" son of the German-American anthropologist, Franz Boas, also the father of modern anthropology. Rollo, born in Manitoba around 1909, trained as an Anglican vicar but was heavily influenced by the Oxford Group. He married Kay Harrington, a nurse, and the couple joined the Columbia Coast Mission in 1944, operating the mission boat *Rendezvous* for a decade along the central coast. During the winter, they were based in the northern Gulf Islands. The Boases, through the Oxford Group principles, promoted a spiritual path of healing that wasn't exclusively Christian. They accepted that healing could come through other spiritual traditions. This was almost as radical a Western idea as Rollo's grandfather's observation that race was not a determiner of cultural or intellectual superiority. Kay Boas's path would undoubtedly have crossed Wa'xaid's as they moved up and down the coast during that decade. They weren't to meet again for another half-century but instantly recognized one another in 2004 on the *Spirit of Endeavour*, one of the environmental discovery voyages organized by Adventure Canada for which Wa'xaid, Kay Boas and David Suzuki were all brought aboard as teachers.

85 Wa'xaid returned to Kitamaat Village permanently around 1967. It was at this time he fell in love with Patricia (Mamie or Mae) Williams, the daughter of Charles and Sadie Williams, members of a high-ranking

Haisla family. Alcohol was an ever-present fixture in Wa'xaid's life at the time, as it was in Mae's. Their four children, born between 1967 and 1970 (Rhoda, Maudie, Joyce and Cecil Jr.), were all born to parents struggling with alcoholism.

86 The bragging beaver story is actually a waterfall of stories, each one cascading over the other. One of the big clans of the Xenaksiala is the Beaver Clan. There are obvious attractions to beavers: their thick fur in a cold land, their tender meat available year-round, and their large incisor teeth that make fine carving tools. An Xenaksiala man, the late James Robertson, wrote down the story of the origin of the Beaver Clan. The story must be millennia old, as it is set in a treeless time, before the arrival of western redcedar on the coast, when paths ran everywhere, even the length of Gardner Canal, because the people had no canoes. The story involves a man, who comes upon a redcedar that reveals its qualities, and his wife Qulun, a Xenaksiala woman who takes the form of the first beaver to help shape the first canoe. Qulun is the name for beaver.

In ecological terms, beaver are keystone species – like the keystone of an arch in a bridge, without which the bridge collapses. In the Kitlope, the idea of beaver as a keystone species is easy to grasp. Everything from salmon to Wa'xaid relies on beaver. When there is no barricade or roots to hold it, soil and mud near a river only have one destination, downwards to the sea. Once soil is barricaded by a beaver's dam, however, willow quickly establishes, and then the soil builds to the point that redcedars can root themselves, often around marooned driftwood. Once growing, a redcedar must thrive for a mere 300 years before it can be carved into a canoe, which the people do by using the teeth of beaver. If any being should brag about its superlative talents, it probably should be the beaver.

87 Godfrey Knutson is listed as a miner/prospector from Butedale in the *Annual Report of the Minister of Mines of the Province of British Columbia for the Year Ended 31st of December, 1930*. That year he has claims listed as Bute and Bute No. 2, which he co-owned with Albert Lund and were opposite the Butedale cannery on the south side of Butedale Bay. No record of a Kowesas claim was found in the annual reports between 1906 and 1930, but Kemano River was claimed in 1906 by Mr. Darkin and Mr. Pocklington of Victoria for its copper and molybdenite, while Kiltuish Inlet was claimed in 1920 by James Hickey for gold. The altercation

in the Kowesas appears to have gone unrecorded by the Ministry of Mines – not the first time in the rush for gold.

88 Mountain goats are extraordinary animals with the ability to endure the harshest of winter conditions in the mountains. They scale cliffs along tiny ledges and survive on virtually any kind of plant food, including bark and lichens. Snowpack will drive them down to sea level in the winter, but in the spring, they retreat to safety from their many predators to alpine meadows that are close to their escape paths on the cliffs. Watching for goats in the Kitlope requires its own kind of stamina: holding a pair of binoculars up for hours to a tilted head as you scan the cliffs for the characteristic whitish-yellow dot against the black-grey granite. Goats are discernible from white dots of snow by their yellowish tinge, but only just. They shed their long guard hairs and thick underfur for a shorter summer coat. Picking up the wool from their trails was an important task for weavers. Goats are a leftover from the time of the Bering bridge; their closest cousins are the goat-antelopes of the Himalayas and southeast Asia. BC has half the world's population of mountain goats, and the Kitlope constitutes an important sanctuary for them.

89 See Wa'xaid's story "Stone Hunter: T'ismista."

90 The logs that Wa'xaid loaded were mainly coming out of Kemano, Wa'xaid's own *wa'wais*. Once the hundred-ton bundles were towed to the Kitimat dock, they were loaded onto trucks that drove the 75-kilometre highway that Wa'xaid had helped survey, then to the Skeena sawmills that he had laboured at. Finally, they were shipped down the railway line that he had helped build. There wasn't too much of the journey of those logs that didn't rely at some stage on the sweat equity of Wa'xaid.

When he worked for the Skeena mills, Wa'xaid made friends with a young man called Bill Munro. Munro was the person he recommended to take the supervisor position, which required the ability to read and write. His friendship with Bill Munro lasted a lifetime, and when they needed two old-growth cedars for the replica G'psgolox poles (see his story, "Return of the G'psgolox Pole"), Wa'xaid went to Munro, now high up in management of the Skeena mill.

When the Eurocan pulp mill started up in 1970, Wa'xaid moved to the docks loading pulp. He was there until his heart attack forced him to retire in 2001. He was never fired for his advocacy for the Kitlope. Nine years later, Eurocan closed with some very good assets to sell, a strategic dock at a deep-water port and a good chunk of real estate for the next extractive industry – liquefied natural gas.

91 One hundred fifty years ago, a germ war was waged through small-pox. With so many dying during the summer of 1862, anyone left either starved or went looking for food. It is remarkable that any cultural knowledge survived the chaos. Wa'xaid tells the story of the return of the young warrior to his home because it is the story that brought him back to his valley after a similar assault on culture – the residential schools and ensuing struggle with alcohol. In that 150 years between smallpox and today, Crab River has been a saltery, a steamer stop, a logging camp and a fish camp where Marguerite Demers, the mother of Wa'xaid's first child, was raised. What hasn't changed are the anabatic and katabatic winds. Warm anabatic winds are driven upslope by the warm surface temperatures of the sun-baked mountain slopes. Cold katabatic air also spills down from the glaciated mountains and, because of its density, slides underneath the warm winds. The warm breeze he describes is a phenomenon of the inlet, which can follow a cool wind in quick succession, and the Creator indeed warms you with each alternate breath.

Four: Healing Journey

92 Ethnographer Brian Compton spent 1988 to 1992 with Xenaksiala Elder Gordon Robertson (not to be confused with Haisla Elder Gordon Robinson), recording the rich Xenaksiala relationship with plants. There are many aspects of this relationship from which you can draw parallels to a child and a grandparent. Plants keep you company, they teach you of their uses, they feed you, their medicine heals your body, and they hold the earth and feed the animals. One of the richest plants for stories is Indian riceroot, *xukʷm* (*Fritillaria camschatcensis*). All the species of *Rubus* (blackcaps, thimbleberries and salmonberries) are cultivated and harvested by the Xenaksiala from the time they appear as shoots, which are picked, peeled and eaten like celery, to the harvesting of their berries. The blossoms are full of vitamin C. From a dietary perspective, the mixture of oolichan oil, riceroot and salmonberry is a perfect combination of amino acids, vitamins, carbohydrates, omega oils and proteins. The body would be receptive to this life-giving medicine flooding in after a long cold winter – for Wa'xaid, the long cold winter

was really years of an impoverished diet at the residential schools and during his life as an alcoholic.

93 See Wa'xaid's story "When I First Came Back."

94 Iona Campagnolo won the Skeena riding as a federal Liberal in 1974. Heber Maitland was the chief councillor of the Haisla during her years in office. There are newspaper accounts of the Haisla taking their concerns to the federal government throughout the 1970s but no record of Wa'xaid's request to Her Honour are in the public record. The only surviving letter from Haisla leadership found in Campagnolo's collection is dated May 18, 1978. It is addressed to her fellow minister, the Honourable Hugh Faulkner, and cc'd to her. He was a band councillor at the time (the only time he served in a political capacity) under Maitland, before he stepped down that November for health reasons. Following are excerpts from Maitland's letter, now held in the Iona Campagnolo Fonds (2009.6.13.17.063 Indian and Northern Affairs/Indian Bands, Councils and Reserves/Kitamaat) in Northern BC Archives, listing the historic concerns:

> The stability and direction that people normally find in their culture and traditions are seriously endangered in our society; our old ways have been scorned and even outlawed by Canadian society; our chiefs and elders have had their authority undermined; and instead an alien system incompatible with and often hostile to, our own ways, has been imposed on us.... The land and resource base will, we believe, enable us to maintain ourselves in some of our old occupations, re-establish ourselves in others now lost to us, and gain entry into a number of new ones. The most important of our traditional occupations covers our subsistence economy: the taking, processing, distribution and consumption of our native foods. This aspect of our way of life remains highly significant, both from a nutritional and a cultural standpoint. A study of traditional foodstuffs conducted last year at Kitimaat revealed that fishing and hunting and gathering continue to play a vital part in the diet and household economics of all elements of our society, no matter what age, occupation or social position. It is important to us that this way of life continue, yet it is under threat from a number of directions. In the past several years there has been a marked decline in the both the quantity and quality of some of the foods taken near Kitimaat. Industrial pollution, damage to habitat,

severe competition from sportsmen and increasingly restrictive regulations combine to make continuation of our traditional gathering ways more and more difficult.

Iona Campagnolo has been widely honoured for her work on women's and human rights. She was celebrated during the 150th anniversary of Confederation, as Stephen Hume wrote in the February 17, 2017, *Vancouver Sun*, for her "profound passion for her province, its environment and its cultural diversity." Raised as a child on the Skeena in Prince Rupert by fish-cannery workers, she was the first woman to hold the Ministry of Sports portfolio, the first female president of the federal Liberal party and the first female lieutenant-governor.

95 Huge trees in floodplains are, like Wa'xaid, survivors. Typically, impermanence reigns in a floodplain like the spring blush of the wild Nootka rose. The spring freshets reach velocities and forces that make Alcan's efforts to move Sand Hill seem almost puny. Sand and silt are deposited; then they are taken away. The banks are in a constant flux of wax and wane. Thickets of berries wash away and re-establish, if water and bears disperse their seeds. When a nurse log comes to rest on these shifting sands, it is like a small raft upon which trees can safely take root. A young tree might anchor itself through the rotting nutrients of the log into the shifting banks, spread its roots far and wide and tap into one of the most powerful life forces ever documented on Earth. Sitka Spruce put on incredible growth rings, which is why they were so highly prized as a strong but light wood for airplane construction and mine props. They were highly graded during the Second World War.

96 Alcoholism kills slowly and selectively. There are genetic, social and childhood-trauma predispositions for the disease. Wa'xaid struck unlucky on all three. Alcohol started another systemic addiction: colonial governments became dependent on revenues from the sale of alcohol. Alcohol is the leading cause for hospitalizing people in all of BC, especially when you add in the indirect effects of brawls, mental illness and impaired-driving injuries.

97 Wa'xaid has witnessed first hand the disease among those working in isolated industrial camps where money is flush. The Gillette effect – named for the oil and coal boomtown of Gillette, Wyoming, which experienced rapid resource development in the 1970s – includes high rates of drug and alcohol addiction, violence, car accidents and sexual assaults on the vulnerable, all associated with the hypermasculinity

of predominantly male, resource-extraction camps. No country that bases its economy on large-scale exploitation of resources is going to advertise this problem. Wa'xaid, as a speaker and sponsor for AA, has supported hundreds of men in his life, Indigenous and white, most in anonymity. One who has spoken about his disease is Chris Cook from Alert Bay, a 'Namgis fisherman who went on to become the leader of the Native Brotherhood, fighting fish farms in his territory from the 1980s until this writing.

98 Kemano Completion Project (KCP) was part of Alcan's long-term plans for expanding its production of aluminum. The aluminum-production process is an electricity vampire, so to expand, Alcan needed to extract more water from the Nechako Reservoir, which meant more water would be released down the Kemano River. Both changes in water flow would have impacts on the salmon of the Fraser River (as the Nechako is a major river of the Fraser system) and the oolichon of the Kemano River. The battle between fisheries and Alcan went on for seven years until the 1987 Settlement Agreement was signed. No First Nations were involved in those discussions, nor were they brought into the steering committee the following year when KCP loomed on the horizon. The Department of Fisheries and Oceans, wanting to avoid another protracted battle, gathered Alcan and the provincial Ministry of Environment, Lands and Parks to "ensure environmental and fisheries protection." (See Lorna R. Barr, Peter A. Larkin, and J. Alistair McVey, *Kemano Completion Project Review* [BC Utilities Commission, 1994].) Back at the Kemano River in 1984, fisheries consultants Envirocon anticipated a large increase of 103 cubic metres per second with a recommendation to lower capacity during the oolichan spawning season. One million small fish were going to courageously swim between a billion-dollar company and a quarterly return. The Haisla weren't buying the promises.

99 In about 1987 the people of Kitamaat Village, under Gerald Amos's leadership, went to find out was going on with the people of the Nechako, the Cheslatta – their trading partners at the end of a grease trail. The Cheslatta were as much in the dark as they had been in the 1950s. At that time, the first they knew about Alcan was when the Kenney Dam caused the river to flood their homes and traplines. The social cost to the Cheslatta was undefinable: the dam was another tool

of genocide. The settlement for the Cheslatta only came half a century later, when almost all the people directly affected were dead.

In the spring of 1989, Kitamaat Village Elders and councillors prepared their affidavits for an injunction to halt Alcan's KCP and any other megaprojects that threatened the people's way of life. Chief Maitland had filed a comprehensive land claim for the Haisla back in 1978, but little had progressed with it. On May 11, Amos told Dan Gilmore at the *Northern Sentinel*, the local newspaper, that the band was "using a peashooter to challenge a billion-dollar project." But this peashooter would have startling range and power. It kicked off a campaign to raise awareness that ultimately triggered a two-year review under the Utilities Commission Act. Wa'xaid, Gerald Amos and other Haisla Elders took their objections to the KCP on the road, at the same time as the Kitlope story, and they shot the pea right out of the arena. The KCP was never completed, for many reasons, not least of which were the public objections raised.

100 See Wa'xaid's story "Five Rivers of Oolichan."

101 Once the Haisla got their foot in the door to talk about oolichan, some things started to change. The year 1989 was good for raising awareness, as the Boston Men arrived at this time, along with their independent sources of funding for research. One of the first things the Haisla did was hire some independent fish scientists to work with their members who knew the oolichan the best, like Wa'xaid. The baseline data that was captured in the 1984 report about the oolichan returns would be instrumental in arguing their case with Eurocan. Even subtle changes in river fluctuations could have profound impacts on the poor-swimming oolichan. Wa'xaid's observations were correct. The data also showed that distinct populations develop their own adaptations to their rivers. (This fact worked in the Haisla's favour for the timing of the logging plans of the Kitlope.) Over time, the communication between Alcan and the Haisla allowed the flows to be regulated to the point that the oolichan could successfully spawn. The Kemano was monitored by Alcan between 1988 and 2004. The oolichan returns plummeted in 1988, and by 1999 there were no returns. In 2003 there was a single small return, and then the population went back down to negligible levels until 2008, when the population started to return in high numbers.

102 Sasquatch, or *bek'ʷus*, is the Haisla "monster" most captured by Western imaginations. Haisla author Eden Robinson's *Monkey Beach* brought

her contemporary Haisla storytelling skills to the old story of *bek'ʷus*. The title of her book echoes the English local place name, referring to the resemblance of *bek'ʷus* to a monkey. The Haisla place name is Q'waq'waqsiyas. An encounter at Misk'uk'w is included in Wa'xaid's telling of the story of Billy Hall. Billy Hall was a skillful Xenaksiala healer. He was born sometime around 1860 and married Susan (no last name), who gave birth to Simon Hall in 1899. Simon married Amelia Duncan, who gave birth to Kenny and Simon Hall Jr. (hereditary chiefs of the Kitlope who supported the Kitlope campaign), both from the Eagle Clan in the Kitlope.

103 One of the graves, inches away from being washed into the sea in 1993, was that of Xenaksiala healer Billy Hall. In 2017 John Pritchard told me that Jean-Louis LeMay was a manager of the power operation at Kemano and "a reasonable human being." His "reasonable" solution was to support Wa'xaid's recommendation to build up a bulwark and shore up the burial ground and village site. The pole was christened Nanakila for the watchman.

Nanakila is a striking pole with oolichan swimming up from the bottom chased by seal, sea lion and grizzly; beaver and eagle are at the top – the eagle has flashing mirror eyes. In between, an empty part of the pole accounts for the loss of wildlife due to industrial activity or the unknown future of industrial occupation – a river devoid of oolichan and the culture of life they support. Coca Cola heiress, and friend of Wa'xaid, Glenn Fuller donated money for the pole, as did Michael Northrup for the Rockefeller brothers. Henry Stewart carved it. Many assumed it was an assertion of sovereignty at Kemano by the Haisla, who had launched their injunction against Alcan that spring. On October 25, 1989, Dan Gilmore of the *Northern Sentinel* quoted Amos speaking to the Haisla intention at the pole raising in the late fall of 1989: "Nanakila is one measure of our effort to challenge all concerned. It will stand as our candle, a noble and reflective expression of conscience."

104 The Nanakila pole was raised at Kemano in the fall of 1989.

105 Ceceila Cashore Reekie's story:

I had my first-born son, David, in 1987. Holding my son for the first time, was very powerful for me as it was the first person to whom I had been biologically connected. It was then that I understood the importance of that connection and decided to search for my birth mum. I applied through Parent Finders in 1989. My mum had been registered with Parent Finders for a number of years and so the match was made almost immediately. They called the following day with Margeurite's phone number. I was still living in Langley and she was living in Delta. I had grown up within a half hour of my birth mother. I called her and we made arrangements for myself, Dave my husband, and baby Dave to meet her that night. We spent the evening sharing stories and pictures and at some point I asked her about my dad. I am very lucky, because she was honest and gave me his name.

That night, I went home and phoned my parents, John and Sharon Cashore. I had promised that I would call them and let them know how the reunion went. In that phone call, I mentioned that my birth father's name was Cecil Paul from Kitamaat. I asked Dad if he had a connection to Kitamaat because I wanted to find out if he knew someone who might know him. My mum said: "Aunt Louisa's maiden name was Paul and she came from Kitamaat. I wonder if they are related?" She said that she was going to phone Aunt Louisa that night. We hung up the phone and Mum called Aunt Louisa and explained that I had just found her birth mum and that her birth dad was Cecil Paul of Kitamaat. Mum asked her if he was any relation. I don't think Aunt Louisa said anything at first and that she would have to call my parents back. Then Aunt Louisa called Cecil that night and asked him if he had had a baby girl in 1963 and he said: 'Yes.' Aunt Louisa said to Cecil: 'Well I know who she is and she is now looking for you.' Aunt Louisa called my parents back and told them that Cecil was her older brother and, yes, he would be willing to meet Cecelia.

Cecil was scheduled to travel down for a doctor's appointment and Aunt Louisa said she would travel with Cecil. I met them in a hotel room in Vancouver. I was anxious, nervous but excited at reconnecting with Aunt Louisa and meeting my birth dad. I made my way to the hotel room, with my arms full of albums and pictures and things, and knocked on the door. Aunt Louisa answered and after greeting her I noticed that Cecil wasn't in the room. I asked her: 'Where is he?' And Aunt Louisa said: 'He is pretty nervous, so he went out for a walk.' We were sharing pictures and chatting when there was a knock on the door. I couldn't see the door from where I was, but I heard Cecil ask Aunt Louisa in their language, if I was there? She said, yes. He came around the corner and didn't say a word. He walked up, gave me a hug and the very first then spoke: 'Be proud of who you are and where you come from.' Then I knew; I had found my way back to my family.

Cecil, Aunt Louisa and I spend the afternoon sharing pictures, stories and talking about our lives and then I took them out to Coquitlam to meet my [adopted] parents, John and Sharon, and my husband and son. We stopped en route for a bouquet of flowers for my mum. When we arrived at the house I grew up in, we gathered up in the living room. To watch my parents meet my birth father and reconnect with their dear friend, Aunt Louisa, is an unforgettable memory. My son was standing over on one side with his dad, when he let his hand go and went over and took Cecil's hand. It was a symbol of connection that was beyond explanation. One of the reasons I wanted to do the search was so that the next generation would know who they were. It was also then that I realized that I had gained three sisters and a brother. Somehow Cecil magically managed to get all of us into a circle as he spoke to my parents to assure them that: 'They weren't going to lose a daughter but the family was just expanding.

106 Before John Cashore met Wa'xaid in 1989, he served three years as an elected New Democratic Party (NDP) member of the provincial legislature. He was in opposition for the first couple of years as the critic for Social Services, then Environment. He had travelled up around that time to Prince Rupert with his wife Sharon to visit their old friends, whom their kids referred to as Uncle Murray and Auntie Louisa Smith. John Cashore told the story that "Louisa and Murray had been up to the Kitlope and they had all these pictures there with her brother – this was before the connection had been made. You could just tell when they got talking about the Kitlope what a beautiful place it was, what a powerful feeling, and that they just loved this place."

One of his duties as Environment critic was to chair a committee on sustainable development – a heady topic at the time. The United Nations' Brundtland Commission on Sustainable Development had come out in 1987, proposing 12 per cent of the land base be set aside for conservation. With the Convention on Biodiversity in Rio looming on the horizon, John's caucus was stepping up to be the very first signatory. The leader of the opposition and his colleagues had lots of shared personal interests in sustainability, and John found himself part of an exciting team. Into this busy milieu in the summer of 1989, his daughter Cecelia contacted her birth parents.

John Cashore first met with the Haisla delegation on January 28, 1993. He was still Environment minister at the time and brought Dan Miller, minister of Forests, with him. At the meeting, they agreed to jointly sponsor two public workshops in the spring about the Kitlope. Over the next year, John transitioned from the Ministry of the Environment to his next appointment as minister of Aboriginal Affairs. (Moe Sihota, an ally and ambitious, was moved into the Ministry of the Environment as minister.) Premier Harcourt had wanted John, with his background in Aboriginal relations with the Church, to take on this portfolio. Bob Peart, his ministerial assistant, pledged to keep the two offices linked in terms of protected areas, as they all involved First Nations. There wasn't much to not like in the proposal. The Haisla were asking for a million acres to be protected, which would boost the provincial percentage up a whole percent in one transaction. There was strong community support, even from the sportspeople and unions. There were just two hurdles left: West Fraser and the issue of compensation for relinquishing a lease on this vast Tree Farm Licence 41 worth millions, and the fact that the main spokesperson for the Haisla was the father of the minister's child.

On February 22, 1994, the Haisla put on a big feast for the Kitlope. The *Northern Sentinel* newspaper reported, "Haisla elder Cecil Paul also spoke to an attentive audience about his willingness to do anything to protect the Kitlope from logging. Paul, who was born in the Kitlope, said he welcomes the world to come and see the Kitlope and learn from it." At this time, West Fraser was still telling the press that their five-year management plan included logging the Kitlope. The provincial government was still reviewing its protected-area plan but would provide a decision within the year. Sometime between February 22 and August, West Fraser decided to donate the Kitlope allocation from Tree Farm Licence 41. Hank Ketcham, owner of West Fraser/Eurocan, spoke in April 2017 about his understanding of the gift:

It is a matter of public record but around 125,000 cubic metres of an annual cut. We relinquished our right and did not ask for compensation. This wasn't a business transaction, but we wouldn't have done this if it had significantly eroded our timber supply for the mill. We had 100 employees. It would have made us millions of dollars but we felt we could run the mills without it. The public's perception was changing, our perception was changing. We were in a unique position to do something good here, it wouldn't hurt our employees. In fact, they got some benefit of the social and environmental benefits and pride in the company.

Of that time, John Cashore told me, "West Fraser gave up the timber rights for the area and this wasn't something that was done lightly or without a certain amount of diplomatic to'ing and fro'ing. Maybe some of the scars on my back come out of that time." In August 1994 the Province and the Haisla Nation announced that the Kitlope would be fully protected and jointly managed.

107 In the end it was Moe Sihota, in his capacity as minister of the Environment, who signed the initial government-to-government agreement on the Kitlope in 1994. John Cashore was in the Khutzemateen, announcing its protection with Prince Philip and chief of the Gitsi'is, Buddy Helene. He had followed the Kitlope closely to the end, though. In September 2015 John told me that the decision to leave the Kowesas out of the agreement was a political compromise: "We weren't able to get the portion in the Kowesas, but what we did manage to do was really a strong step in the right direction. After that there were delegations from Kitamaat on a fairly regular basis coming down." One of the Kitamaat delegation was John Pritchard, who assisted with the detailed two-year-long negotiations on behalf of the Haisla to create a co-managed conservancy area, a new designation (a "conservancy") insisted upon by the Haisla that prioritized the cultural laws and management of the land. The final Kitlope Agreement was signed February 16, 1996. Kowesas was left out of the original agreement, but the moratorium has never come off the valley. When I asked Hank Ketcham about the Kowesas, he had no recollection of it, although he hadn't been the owner of the licence for six years.

Five: More Good Journeys in the Magic Canoe

108 Cecelia's welcome-home ceremony came a year after the protection of the Kitlope. An invitation was issued by the Haisla to those who had worked on its protection, which included John Cashore, in his political capacity, and West Fraser. Cecelia was also given her grandmother Clara's name and button blanket at the ceremony: *Nuyem dzeets 'iksdu-qʷia*, which means "Code of the Eagle."

109 The United Church is exactly 87 steps away from Wa'xaid's house in Kitamaat through the salmonberry bushes.

110 One of the under-reported economic stories of the coast is the Guardian Watchmen Program. The program, born in Haida Gwaii, and adopted by the Haisla in the 1990s and most of the coastal nations since then, became a full-blown Coastal Guardian Watchmen Network in 2006 to coordinate all their activities. The network's slogan is "We are the eyes and ears of the coast" at a time when government stewardship presence on the coast is virtually non-existent. The provincial agenda since 2001 to deregulate and substitute the "eyes and ears" of government oversight with a system called professional reliance (referred to by critics as the fox guarding the chicken coop), has left the seas and land vulnerable to poaching, pollution and illegal activities; it has also left the field wide open to resume traditional stewardship activities.

Watchmen's duties have increased every year. They monitor for illegal and dangerous activities: trophy hunting of grizzly, illegal sport fishing, oil spills, injured marine mammals, poaching, dumping of garbage, illegal logging, looting of archaeological sites, forest fires, lost tourists and natural emergencies. Watchmen also collect their own scientific information on terrestrial and marine life, and archaeological and recreational activity on behalf of their nations to help implement land- and marine-use agreements. Funding for the Watchmen Programs comes from interest earned on the $120 million Coast Opportunities Fund, which was generated by environmental organizations and First Nations, and matched by provincial and federal funds for the Great Bear Rainforest Agreement. There are now various training programs that translate into what a fisheries officer or park warden job would require.

111 When the Davis Plan was introduced in 1971, the Native fishing fleet had already declined by half in less than seven years. The commercial fleets were blowing locals out of the water, while stocks were declining. It was the final nail in the coffin for small-scale Indigenous fishermen; it favoured those with capital who could improve the efficiency of their boats to meet increased operating standards. Through the buy-back program, the Department of Fisheries and Oceans reduced the number of boats, as those who couldn't afford to upgrade had no alternative but to sell. They also consolidated the fleet by giving larger boats the ability to obtain rights to fish in other areas.

The "grandfather clause" that Wa'xaid refers to is the special

Indigenous licence that the Department of Fisheries and Oceans created in response to the issue of the rapid decline in Aboriginal fishers. It was a token, inexpensive licence for existing boat owners, which gave them the right to fish but not the ability to sell the licence – hence "grandfather." Under another federal program, called the Indian Fisherman's Assistance Program, there was some capital available for Indigenous fishermen to upgrade, but again this program favoured existing boat owners who had the down payment necessary to get in on the scheme.

Fishing policy did not change substantially with the Mifflin Plan in the 1990s, which replaced the Davis Plan with the same results. On January 20, 1998, Corky Evans, then minister of Agriculture, Fisheries and Food for BC, summed up the two world views of fisheries at a standing committee for the House of Commons on fish:

> The economists argue that when the fishing fleet is too large the marginal fishers should be eliminated, and hence the Davis plan and then the Mifflin plan and the placing of huge costs on the acquisition of a licence to go fishing…. For example, if you were an economist studying west coast salmon you would say that total salmon harvests are generally increasing. But if you're a resident of Bella Bella or a DFO biologist, you would say that people are starving because the ecosystem that once made them commercial fishers and processors is wounded. If you're an economist, you would say that the Mifflin plan to reduce the fleet to increase the viability of the remaining operators was a perfectly rational response to a changing technology and market conditions. If, however, you were a resident of Ahousat, or maybe a lot of the people in this room, you would say that it's the elimination of half the jobs in your community.

112 With ancestors so ever present in Wa'xaid's life, it wasn't surprising that he and David Suzuki sailed together down the northwest coast on the HMS *World Discoverer* two weeks shy of two centuries after Captain Vancouver brought HMS *Discovery* into Gardner Canal. Those aboard and their aspirations, however, couldn't have been more different from each other. This time a Japanese-Canadian and a Xenaksiala man, apparently having nothing more in common than having survived Canadian detention camps, were sailing to share a vision of protecting a culture and landscape.

With the next political cycle, fish-farm expansion was once again a hot item. Suzuki was aware of what was coming down the line and turned his foundation's sights on getting a broad review of the science and alternative views to that of the industry boosters. 2001 was a busy year for reviews of finfish aquaculture. The federal Auditor General's Report came out in February, the Standing Senate Committee Report came out in June, and the David Suzuki Foundation–funded Leggatt Inquiry came out in November. Stuart Leggatt, a retired judge, was given independence to hear and review the evidence.

The northern villages were not on the inquiry circuit, but the Native Brotherhood spoke for the coastal fishermen. Chris Cook (whom Wa'xaid inspired to join AA), of the Namgis First Nation, was an important witness as leader of the Native Brotherhood. Several of his observations were cited in the report: that Aboriginal bands were left with no choice but fish farms because of erosion of their fishing opportunities. Cook spoke about the divide-and-conquer tactics and his people "being used as pawns by the aquaculture industry.... I'm tired of sending letters. I'm tired of talking. I hope my people stand up and start to fight." (See *Clear Choices, Clean Waters: Leggatt Inquiry into Salmon Farming in British Columbia, Reports and Recommendations*, April 2001, pp. 10–11.)

The moratorium was lifted on new locations for fish farms, and the five-year battle (that Wa'xaid refers to) was waged in the northern communities where there were still livelihoods to be made in fishing. By 2008 a total ban for the north coast (north of Klemtu) was placed on open-net fish farms.

113 The fish farm issue raised its head for the Haisla Nation somewhat abstractly in the late 1980s. Atlantic salmon open-net fish farms arrived on the coast in a fairly innocuous way in the early 1980s – mom-and-pop operations around Vancouver Island and the Sunshine Coast. There were just ten farms in 1984, but within a couple of years, the industry had grown tenfold, although only the northern village of Klemtu, which Wa'xaid refers to in his story, started looking into the business. The tiny remote community of Klemtu had lost all its fish boats to the Davis and Mifflin Plans (see note 112). It had an existing fish-processing plant that was standing empty, and the community had few alternatives. A moratorium on further expansion of fish farms was put in place in October 1986, while a commission led by David Gillespie explored some of the stickier issues of growth. That report came out in the winter

of 1987 and included some Haisla input. The leadership showed concern for the impact on their own fishery and the commercial fishery, as well as environmental impacts, but many families were now without fish boats or a livelihood, and this raised the hope for an alternative. The "turning point" for the north that Wa'xaid refers to came when the scientific studies started to show the long-term impacts on native salmon populations.

114 In 1995 the Nuxalk (Bella Coola people) hereditary chiefs led by Nuximlayc (Lawrence King, Chief Pootlass) took a stand and blockaded their most sacred valley, Ista, against the logging company Interfor. The chiefs were jailed, but they issued a declaration of Nuxalk Sovereignty. They lost their last run of oolichan in 1998.

115 In the opening scene of the NFB television documentary *Totem: Return of the G'psgolox Pole* the camera pans the G'psgolox pole from the mythical sea-dwelling grizzly at the bottom, up the body of Asoalget, half-animal/half-man and ending with Tsooda – the magic man – at the top. Tsooda had been looking down onto visitors of the Swedish Museum of Ethnography for 77 years. The public Xenaksiala story of the G'psgolox pole starts in 1872 when it was commissioned at Misk'usa, where the remaining Kitlope people had converged after enduring smallpox. Wa'xaid tells his own version of the story that is more about other peoples' roles than his own: his sister Louisa, Gerald, John Pritchard, Louise Barbetti and his brother Dan, as well as the role of the owner of the pole and name, Chief G'psgolox. Wa'xaid also names the central hero of the story as Annie Paul, his granny. The case was of interest to the museum profession because not only was it the first totem pole successfully repatriated voluntarily by a foreign museum to a First Nations community but it was notable for being such a positive experience for the European institution. Even though they were losing an artifact, the Swedes gained a window on a living culture and the chance to reconnect the public with the owners, storytellers and contemporary carvers – artists who were related to the original carvers. Museum attendance went up, and renewal flowed both ways. It was a typical Haisla solution to a seemingly intractable problem of contested ownership. The teachings, of course, were re-attributed to the pole itself – a living being.

Montserrat Gonzales, who Wa'xaid says found the pole, was an archivist for the Kitimat Museum and Archives in the late 1980s and early 1990s. She had learned of the job while working in the University of British Columbia art history library with June Pritchard (John Pritchard's wife) when she was a master's student. The first trip to Finland that the Haisla made in the winter of 1991 to negotiate with the Finnish shareholders over their trees was also a trip to see the pole for the first time. It was next door, at the Swedish Museum of Ethnography.

There were certainly no policy barriers in 1928 when the Swedish Consul in Prince Rupert, Olof Hansson, approached the Indian agent for the region, Ivan Fougner, to purchase a pole for his country. Fougner obliged and wrote his department, recommending the purchase since "chances are that the pole, if not removed, after some time would fall down and be destroyed." (See *G'psgolox Pole: Return and Renewal*, Nanakila Institute, 2006, for the quoted material here and in the rest of this note).

On January 11, 1928, the department granted Fougner an export licence, given that "the Indian reserve was uninhabited and very isolated" and "provided that the Indian owners are willing to dispose of it." Although no one was there that winter, it wasn't uninhabited. Still, the pole was cut down and taken away to Stockholm, where it was erected outside the Museum of Ethnography for six months. Wa'xaid was born shortly afterwards, and Annie Paul impressed upon her grandson, as soon as he could understand, that permission to take it had not been granted.

The pole then spent the next 40 years in an old storeroom in Stockholm. It was moved then treated for dry rot in a storeroom alongside the ancient warship *Wasa*. *Wasa* would become an important leverage tool in the Haisla argument for the pole. The Haisla stated that if they had taken *Wasa* without permission, the Swedes might feel the same way they did about their pole.

In 1980 the Swedes built a special climate-controlled building designed to accommodate the pole, and there it stood until the Xenaksiala/Haisla delegation arrived to see the pole for the first time in December 1991. The protection of the Kitlope and the return of the pole were certainly linked in the international press, and the Swedes' negotiating room was narrowing. In February 1994, the Swedish government agreed to "gift" the pole back to Kitamaat Village, but it directed the Kitimat Museum to ensure that the Haisla would preserve the pole. Perceptions of what a gift was, who the gift was for and why there were conditions on the gifts filled the next three years of negotiation but also triggered the Haisla to practice "creativity [in] the negotiation process."

The Haisla were back on the plane to Sweden again in 1997 – this time with Wa'xaid.

Wa'xaid won many Swedish hearts even as he raised the expectation for an unconditional release of the pole back to its rightful owners. His determination may have lost Western negotiating ground, but it gained ground in terms of Haisla relationship building. While the Haisla group was in Sweden, they came up with the idea of carving the replicas. When the delegation returned, Nanakila and Ecotrust Canada started raising funds for two replica poles – one for Misk'usa and one for Sweden.

The replica pole, carved in Kitamaat, was raised in Misk'usa during the summer of 2000, and the sister pole was sent to Sweden with carver Henry Robertson and his nephews, Derek and Barry Wilson, who would do the finishing touches. From start to finish, the pole negotiations between the Haisla and the Swedes lasted 15 years. In 2005 the Swedes finally conceded and dropped their conditions. The Haisla took one more delegation over in March 2006 for the raising of the replica pole. Wa'xaid and Cecil Junior went for the ceremony.

Finally released by the Swedes, the pole crossed the Atlantic, went through the Panama Canal and ended up at the University of British Columbia Museum of Anthropology on April 26, 2006, for its official welcome by Wa'xaid's brother Dan, Chief G'psgolox. The Vancouver Foundation also had a big gala to celebrate the return for National Aboriginal Day. The pole arrived in Kitamaat Village on July 1, 2006, to another village celebration and there it lay, first in the new school, then at Kitimat City Centre Mall for five years, before going to its final resting place on September 19, 2011 – in the rainforest from whence it came.

116 Brian Falconer sold the *Maple Leaf* to Kevin Smith in 2003 and joined Raincoast Conservation Foundation to assist with its research and advocacy for the protection of the coast. He refitted and captained the research vessel *Achiever*, which carried research crews on salmon, grizzlies, seabirds, whales and wolves. *Achiever* has travelled over 30,000 kilometres up and down the coast, conducting inventory of marine mammal and seabird populations in the path of tankers, tracking the seasonal movements of grizzlies to get a better determination of populations, and much more. Raincoast also purchased the guiding and outfitting licences for much of the central coast, and Brian has been the de facto guide, leading "shooting" expeditions as required by the licence. To the time of this writing, they have been singularly "unsuccessful"

in shooting a single bear. At the same time, the organization has campaigned using science to end the grizzly trophy hunt. Finally, in December 2017, the last loophole for trophy hunting was closed in BC. Wa'xaid's last trip with Brian was in fact in the autumn of 2017, when with Gerald they took Bruce Hill's ashes to Kitlope Lake.

117 The Haisla have been fighting supertankers since the first proposal to bring a pipeline to Kitimat was put on the table in the mid-1970s. Trans Mountain Corporation, with the backing of five US refining companies, put in a proposal to build a pipeline from Edmonton to Kitimat. Trans Mountain pulled the proposal at the end of 1976, arguing high costs, but a new proposal was submitted to the National Energy Board shortly after by Kitimat Pipeline Ltd.

The public pressure helped. In a letter to her colleague Minister of Aboriginal Affairs Hugh Faulkner, Iona Campagnolo shared a comment spoken by their prime minister. "He stated that if the Kitimat proposal was just to meet American needs, 'then my attitude is, Why don't they just build a port on their west coast?'" (See Iona Campagnolo to Hugh Faulkner correspondence, May 12, 1978, Iona Campagnolo Fonds, 2009.6.13.30.54 1975-1978 Transport/Marine Transportation/Ports, Harbour and Wharves/Kitimat, UNBC Archives.) The only dissenter on record for scrapping the project in February 1978 appeared to be the mayor of Kitimat.

One generation later, on May 27, 2010, Northern Gateway Pipelines Ltd. submitted its Enbridge Northern Gateway Project Application to the National Energy Board to bring a pipeline from Bruderheim, Alberta, to Kitimat. Markets and the resource had changed; this time the proposal was for Alberta oil and was financed by Chinese refineries looking to ship their bitumen west. The argument of what constituted Canadian versus British Columbia interests became the basis for a prolonged and political battle in which the Haisla were to exert the same arguments they had before, but this time with 30 years of honed legal precedents and scientific data to draw from. Many others with whom the Haisla had forged relationships testified.

The hearings were held in January 2012. On January 9, Joe Oliver, then minister of Natural Resources, claimed on the CBC's *The National* that "radical" environmentalists were being fuelled by "socialist billionaires" from the US intent on "demarketing" Alberta's tar sands. Oliver's "socialist billionaire" outburst stemmed from the blogs and special missives to the *Financial* and *National Posts*, written by Conservative conspiracist Vivian Krause, ex-Conservative party worker and oil patch apologist, fuelled by Conservative political commentator Ezra Levant's "ethical oil" rantings. Among the more puzzling of the outbursts of moral outrage was at the $5,000 donation made by an American charity to a children's summer camp for Heiltsuk First Nations. The fact that underprivileged children from Bella Bella were unlikely to be posing a national threat to economic security seemed to bypass then–Prime Minister Stephen Harper's communications branch.

Gerald Amos kicked off the hearings in Kitamaat on January 20. Merve Ritchie quoted Amos in the *Kitimat Daily Online* that day when Amos told Oliver, "The fact that our conservation leadership has attracted the support of conservation funders should be a source of pride for British Columbians. We do not follow the lead of anyone; we assume and take responsibility for our lands and lead others in that regard." Not surprisingly, Oliver's attempts to distract backfired spectacularly and provided a flurry of activity among journalists to get to the bottom of the real motivation behind this "escapade." What didn't pass unnoticed was Oliver's failure to note that there were ten foreign oil companies registered as intervenors and not a single foreign environmental organization.

The Haisla brought their final 362-page legal argument before the federal and provincial Joint Review Panel in May 2013. Brian Falconer, with Raincoast Conservation Foundation, presented his final written and oral argument on marine safety. Biologist John Kelson also brought his evidence on risk to oolichan populations. Twenty years after the canoe had launched, the paddlers of the Magic Canoe continued to bring their research skills to the Haisla cause for cultural and ecological justice.

118 There have been three LNG projects proposed for Kitimat: the $40-billion LNG Canada (Shell Canada); the $3.5-billion Kitimat LNG (Chevron Corporation), just outside Kitimat at Bish Cove; and a smaller project of floating LNG terminals, Cedar LNG, proposed by the Haisla. The Haisla push for LNG has been spearheaded by Ellis Ross, son of Wa'xaid's friend Russell Ross, with whom he went through Alberni Residential School. Ross Jr. ran on a platform of economic independence, first as an elected councillor, becoming chief councillor for two terms. During those terms he signed a $50-million agreement with Kitimat LNG.

Ross Jr. was handpicked as a candidate for the 2017 election by then–BC Liberal leader Christie Clark, on a pro-industry platform. After winning the Skeena seat, he was briefly appointed the first Indigenous politician to hold a provincial cabinet position, minister of Natural Gas Development. Shortly after, the NDP took power as a minority government. As he told the *Financial Post* on November 16, 2017, "For the first time, since white contact, we were ready to take our place in BC and Canada." However, not all Haisla shared his vision of the future, including Wa'xaid. The divide-and-conquer tactics by Big Oil and Gas permeate every nation, every family and every relationship.

119 Farther north, the nine hereditary chiefs of Lax Kw'alaams Nations signed the Lelu Island Declaration on January 22, 2016. It states, "The undersigned First Nation leaders and citizens of the Nine Allied Tribes of Lax Kw'alaams hereby declare that Lelu Island, and Flora and Agnew Banks are hereby protected for all time, as a refuge for wild salmon and marine resources, and are to be held in trust for all future generations." Louisa's husband, a Tsimshian man, Murray Smith, Algmxaa, is one of the house leaders within the Gitwilgyoots tribe – House of Kelp – which is the territory known geographically as Lelu Island. He was one of the signatories to the declaration. Another was Gerald Amos, who commented on the local Terrace TV news, "I think that the significance of this is that First Nations are coming together and exercising their right to say no to projects like Petronas on Lelu Island that are simply in the wrong spot, and it speaks loudly with respect to the Canadian Environmental Assessment Authority's process and how flawed it is."

The Lelu Island Declaration triggered then-Premier Christy Clark's own famous declaration of sorts on CBC TV, on January 26, 2016: "It's not really about the science; it's not about the fish; it's just about saying no. It's about fear of change; it's about fear of the future. The world is being divided into two: the people that will say no to everything, and the people who want to find a way to get to yes, recognizing that's the way to create jobs, that's how you build a future for your kids, even sometimes when it's really hard."

In the wings of Clark's government, helping "build a future" for her sizeable army of oil and gas investors, boosters and media shills, were two brothers, born in Lax Kw'alaams, anxious to say yes – Calvin and John Helin. Calvin, president, and John, vice-president, of Eagle Spirit Energy Holdings Inc., describe their company as "seeking environmentally-acceptable projects with indigenous people." It was founded in 2012 to establish a First Nations Energy Corridor across northern BC. Calvin

Helin is also an Aboriginal lawyer, entrepreneur and self-described "advocate of indigenous self-reliance." He sits on the Vancouver Board of Trade and is a member of Geoscience BC – whose mandate is to attract mineral and oil and gas exploration – and the Macdonald-Laurier Institute – a right-wing think tank that advocates for industry deregulation. John Helin set up Embark Engineering out of Burnaby, also in 2012, to take on engineering works associated with LNG. The brothers were poised to challenge the seemingly solid position of the Tsimshian, who voted for the third time in May 2015 to reject the Petronas offer of $1 billion dollars. Heavily promoted by pro-industry media, the BC Liberals and the billionaire Luigi Aquilini (who owns the eponymous giant Vancouver construction company and Vancouver Canucks hockey team), the Helins formed a political juggernaut.

On November 20, 2015, John Helin unseated the incumbent chief councillor of Lax Kw'alaams, who didn't support Petronas. Ash Kelly, in a June 23, 2016, article in *Discourse Media*, described what followed in the community as a descent into "one of the most polarized and contentious resource development battles that Canada has witnessed in years." Members of the village, interviewed by Ian Gill (now owner of an independent investigative reporting online media outlet), identified claims of electoral fraud, bullying tactics, discrediting of hereditary chiefs and other divide-and-conquer techniques. (See Ian Gill, "Power Struggle in Northern B.C. Deepens," *Discourse Media*, June 27, 2016.) Hitting home personally for Wa'xaid were the public and unsubstantiated attacks on Donnie Wesley by other alleged leaders of the community, and on Murray Smith, his sister's husband.

The *Financial Post*'s business columnist, Claudia Cattaneo, dubbed "everyone's favourite oil and gas shill" by American Energy News, wrote a column on the failure of LNG projects to advance at the close of 2017. She focussed her article, "'Sickening': First Nations Left Empty-handed as Environmentalist Pressure Kills BC Energy Projects," on the reaction of Ellis Ross and the Helin brothers, and cited Ross: "We were just starting to turn the tide on that opposition to everything," and Helin, "These environmentalists are happy to make a park in somebody else's backyard. Well, screw that. You are talking about people where there is 90 per cent unemployment." On February 13, 2015, Sarah Berman in *The Tyee* quoted Art Steritt of Coastal First Nations when he identified that alliance's position with regard to the "Aboriginal" pipeline company: "literally no First Nation on the coast is in favour of Eagle Spirit [pipeline]."

The cancellation of Petronas's project, according to the company as printed in the July 25, 2017, *Vancouver Sun*, was due to "prolonged depressed prices." However, in May 2018, Petronas switched its investment, along with other foreign investors, to Kitimat's Canada LNG, and the project was greenlighted by the provincial and federal governments in October 2018. At 87, Cecil talked about being too old to fight anymore.

120 There is more than one episode with T'ismista and helicopters. Once a helicopter crashed while taking visitors too close to T'ismista, and it fell into Kitlope Lake.

121 Wa'xaid has buried three daughters: Rhoda in 2002, Joyce in 2016 and Maudie in 2017. Maudie survived three happy years after her heart attack with her husband, Dave. He and Maudie's son Chris accompanied her ashes from Duncan to Kemano. After the ceremony at the burial ground, when the family was leaving in a boat, they witnessed *Gwiiyms moodzill*, the humpback whale, Maudie's Haisla name, sounding off Kemano.

122 Cecelia became the first elected Indigenous school trustee in the Langley School District. Chief Marilyn Gabriel from the Kwantlen Nation signed her nomination papers. Cecelia says of that time: "I was honoured when Chief Gabriel spoke at my swearing in ceremony of her dream to have an Indigenous person at the table and that it was a moment to be proud of. She believes that our children are our most valuable resource." Cecelia became passionate about learning the history of residential schools and participated at the Truth and Reconciliation Commission event in Vancouver. When the report was released in May of 2015, Cecelia travelled back to Ottawa with her friend Kwantlen Elder Josette Dandurand, a residential-school survivor, and Josette's son, Luke Dandurand. On their return from Ottawa, Cecelia, Josette and Luke made a presentation to the Board of Education in Langley and the Langley School District made a public commitment to working towards reconciliation.

On one of Wa'xaid's many visits to see Cecelia, she took him to hear Wab Kinew, the host of *8th Fire* on CBC Television who was speaking at the University of British Columbia Okanagan in Kelowna. During Wab Kinew's talk he shared about how the Elders had kept the fire alive. Wab's father had also gone to residential school. Wa'xaid said, "Yes, we kept the fire alive, but we weren't doing an amazing job of keeping it alive with the next generation." On their drive back to Vancouver, Wab

Kinew tweeted about Wa'xaid: "I met an amazing man this evening who reminds me of my Dad."

123 Wa'xaid's grandson Thomas received the Dla la xii la yewx name on October 26, 2002. He is being raised by his Uncle Cecil Jr., who has moved into the house to look after both his father, Wa'xaid, and his nephew after the death of Thomas's mom Joyce. Three generations of men are in the house. In the family pictures of Thomas growing up, he is never far from his uncle's side – on boats, at the oolichan camp, at the gym.

124 Among the ethnographers, anthropologists and linguists who beat a trail to the Haisla's door, Emmon Bach, like John Pritchard, stands out for many of the people in the village. He was a distinguished linguist and specialist in the Haisla language, finishing a long career as professor emeritus at the University of Massachusetts. He was best known in Kitamaat Village for helping with their goals of capturing and teaching the language. He held true to his Mike Shaw principle: time and resources for research and activities relevant to the community should equal those devoted to academic goals external to the community. In a 2003 article in the *Massachusetts Review* called "Post-colonial Linguistic Fieldwork," Bach described his epiphanic meeting with Haisla speaker Mike Shaw, which led to his departure from the typical, old academic practice of giving little back to the speakers themselves in either support or remuneration: "Mike asked why we were there…. We gave a 15-minute sketch of linguistics, talked about Universal Grammar, about figuring out what the basic structures and possibilities of human language are, about the special reasons why his language was important. When we finished, Mike said, 'Well, I can see all that but…why should we help you, what good will all that do for us?'"

125 The story of Indigenous leaders petitioning the royal family for justice is a long and depressing one of snubs and betrayals. The tradition of clan leadership speaking directly to the royal family stems back to the Royal Proclamation of 1763. Between 1904 and 1906, four BC chiefs petitioned King Edward VII. A Cowichan leader addressed a nephew of the king who was visiting the territory, and three other BC chiefs followed that visit up with a trip to London to put forward their argument.

In 1979 over 200 leaders from the National Indian Brotherhood visited London again to petition Queen Elizabeth II. It was their last hope as constitutional talks of the time threatened once again to leave them out of the discussion. The queen was advised not to meet with them by Prime Minister Joe Clark. When Prince William and Catherine, the Duke and Duchess of Cambridge, came to Bella Bella in 2016, Jessie Housty placed a letter in the couple's hands. Housty is the young woman who runs the Heiltsuk children's camp that former Minister of Natural Resources Joe Oliver saw in 2012 as one of the worst "radical" programs funded by "socialist billionaires." (See CBC's *The National*, January 9, 2012.) She also represented Wa'xaid at the 2013 World Indigenous Network Conference. (See Wa'xaid's story "Back to the Magic Canoe.")

The letter reads:

To the Duke of Cambridge September 26, 2016

Dear Sir,

My name is 'Cúagilákv (Jessie Housty). I am a Heiltsuk Nation citizen, a young mother, and a part of the elected tribal council that greeted you here in Bella Bella.

I hope your visit to our homeland impresses upon you the cultural and ecological richness of this coast, and the strength of the Indigenous peoples who have cared for this place for millennia.

Last Wednesday, I received a call from revered Haisla Nation elder Cecil Paul, who telephoned me from Kitamaat, BC. Cecil has done a great deal of tremendously important work in his lifetime, and inspired emerging leaders of other generations – myself included – to carry on his work of protecting land and culture.

He shared with me that there is something he'd still very much like to see happen in his lifetime. And knowing that you would be visiting us in Bella Bella, our Haisla relative asked me to share a request with you.

Cecil talked to me about the Queen's apology to the Maori people in 1995, in which she personally signed the royal assent for an Act of Parliament acknowledging the injustices our Maori brothers and sisters faced under British colonialism. While these gestures cannot undo past injustices, they represent moments that we can seize to reset our relationships and move forward with clearer hearts.

I am honoured to be asked by Cecil to share this message with you.

Please consider the importance of your family's role in resetting the relationship with the Indigenous peoples of Canada. It would ease our beloved elder's heart to hear such an apology in his lifetime, and if that is not to be, I have promised to keep his request alive until the time is right for it to be acknowledged and fulfilled. This is an important step in beginning to address generations of injustice, and a beautiful and moving step it would be.

Cecil has imparted to us, through a lifetime of stories and teachings, a deep belief that we are strongest when our peoples come together in unity as has been prophesied since time before memory. With the Canadian government's recent focus on reconciliation, this spirit seems to be echoed right from the remote villages of the coast to the halls of parliament in Ottawa.

We hope that spirit catches your heart as well, and that you and your family consider the wish of our gracious and precious elder.

With kind thanks, 'Cúagilákv (Jessie Housty)

126 In the long, slow, perpetual cycle of stories coming from the Magic Canoe of Wa'xaid, the one that returns most frequently is that of the Magic Canoe itself. That story reached an international audience in May 2013. The World Indigenous Network Conference was being held in Darwin, Australia, and 1,400 Indigenous leaders were gathering. Ric Young took Wa'xaid's message of the Magic Canoe along with Jessie Housty to deliver it to the gathering.

Ian Gill reported on the event in *The Tyee* on June 15, 2013, writing about the Indigenous leaders gathered there:

Among them were a number of Canadians, three of whom – perhaps unknown to many in their own country – offered one of the most moving and important lessons of the entire gathering. They appeared on stage together – Jessie Housty, a young indigenous leader from the central coast of British Columbia, holding a canoe paddle in her hands; Ric Young, the Toronto-based founder of The Social Projects Studio and a world-leading architect of social change initiatives; and, looking down on the huge stage and lighting it with a smile every bit as radiant as Nelson Mandela's, indigenous elder Cecil Paul.

Every Indigenous group represented there decorated a paddle with their own art – they assembled the 50-plus paddles for a colourful banner under which Wa'xaid's quote is written: "I was alone in a canoe. But it was a magical canoe because there was room for everyone who wanted to paddle together. The currents against us were very strong. But I believed we could reach our destination and that we had to for our survival."